"Fans of 60s-era spiritualism will love
THE CIRCLE OF LIFE, a memoir/self-help hybrid
by Frank Natale, who seeks to unravel, with
clarity and humor, life's most Gordian knots."

– IndieReader 5 Stars (out of 5)

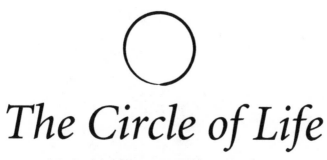

The Circle of Life

A Guide for Conscious Living
in a World of Chaos

FRANK NATALE

M

Library of Congress Control Number: 2021910901

ISBN-13: 978-0-9701443-7-9 (paperback)

ISBN-13: 978-0-9701443-9-3 (e-book)

BISAC: BODY, MIND & SPIRIT / Healing / General / Shamanism

Cover and interior book design by Wendy Saade

Cover photograph "Ibiza Sunrise" by Ralph Cissne

Published by Morgan Road

Other books by Frank Natale:

Relationships for Life

Results: The Willingness to Create

The Wisdom of Midlife

Natale Trance Dance

Trance Dance, the Dance of Life

Table of Contents

Forward viii

Introduction 1

Rites of Passage 5

  1. Birth – The Gifts of Immortality and Magic 19

  2. Coming of Age – A Time for Preparation 30

  3. Separation from the Feminine – A Time for Separation 44

  4. Sexual Initiation – Follow Your Passion 49

  5. Alliance with the Masculine – Pass the Test 55

  6. The Realization of Betrayal – The Illusion of Success 62

  7. Mid-Birth – Birth into Our Power 69

  8. Reconnection with the Feminine –
     Finding the Lost Pieces of Self 76

  9. Initiation into the Truth – Letting Go of Illusions and Lies 83

10. Atonement – Forgiving the Sins of Sun and Moon 92

11. Spiritual Elderhood – Mistress and Master of Many Worlds 96

12. Sharing Your Wisdom – The Return Home 104

13. Beyond Duality – Death, the Final Passage 107

Epilogue 117

About Frank Natale 119

Self-Discovery 121

"Everything, the power of the world, is done in a circle. The sky is round and I have heard the earth is round like a ball and so are all the stars; the wind in its greatest power whirls, birds make their nests in circles for theirs is the same religion as ours. The life of a man is a circle from childhood to adulthood and so it is in everything where power moves."

– Black Elk, Dakota Elder

Forward

I am one among thousands of people throughout the world whose lives continue to be transformed by the wisdom of Frank Natale. With love and compassion, he challenged those willing to move beyond fear and convention to accept responsibility for their lives and, through this process, manifest their dreams into reality. He invited us to be the energized creative force in our lives.

Most importantly, Frank encouraged us to become our own teacher and to laugh at perceived shortcomings. He taught us to make conscious choices, to "stop and be aware" of the self-limitations of our primitive reactive brain. We agreed to acknowledge ourselves, to celebrate the joy of service, and have some fun along the way. "Why not?" he'd say. "That's the point."

June 21, 2002 marked Frank's final passage. This was his birthday and, after a lengthy illness, the day he chose to leave his body. Many friends visited or phoned during those final days. Frank's physical body was failing, but his spirit and mind were sharp. He shared marvelous stories. Those gathered talked and danced into the night. Frank and I discussed The Circle of Life, a years-long project represented in workshops, the album "Rites of Passage" and this manuscript. Because Mid-Birth is often our greatest "crisis" we agreed that section would be published separately. In the years that followed we edited and published *The Wisdom of Midlife*, *Relationships for Life*, *Results: The Willingness to Create*, and *Natale Trance Dance*.

Fresh from my experience in Werner Erhard's seminar The Forum, I met Frank in the mid-80s in Tulsa after his lecture on how creativity manifests results. The room was packed, his presentation brilliant, engaging and at times hilarious. Frank's spiritual point of view aligned with the Zen-centric perspective I gathered from the *Tao Te Ching* and authors such as Kahlil Gibran, J. Krishnamurti, Alan Watts, Carlos

Castaneda and P. D. Ouspensky. We shared many wonderful moments, especially during the 90s when I hosted his workshops in Los Angeles. Like a couple of mischievous teenagers, we explored the aisles of the Bodhi Tree bookstore and Tower Records, enjoyed our fill of sushi and Mexican food. In one particularly magical moment, shrouded in heavy fog beneath the Hermosa Beach pier, we laughed practicing yoga in the sand and chanting Om. Within minutes a breeze stirred and the fog lifted yielding to the promise of a beautiful Southern California day.

Frank's transition, his conscious letting go of this life, was a profound experience that I was honored to witness. *The Circle of Life* is one of Frank's greatest gifts, recounting his extraordinary journey and the wisdom gathered along the way. I promised Frank I would edit this manuscript carefully. His voice speaks clearly in every paragraph. I trust you will discover value on these pages that brings greater clarity and understanding to your life and relationships.

With love and all that truly means,

Ralph Cissne

The Circle of Life

*"Awareness of the Circle of Life helps transform
the experience of crisis into an opportunity
for knowledge and growth."*

Introduction

My life has been filled with countless good times and blessings, but
what I've grown to value most is the wisdom I've received from the
most difficult of life's passages, those that have transformed me and
made me a better person. While they were happening, these troublesome
passages seemed as if they would never be completed. In the end there
has always been the reward of a new and exciting life. I now know there
is a grand scheme, a map of the path we all travel with passages that
give pause to reflect and strip us of our pretense. These passages crucify
our egos and provide time for us to discover what we truly value in life.
I call these transformational rites of passage the Circle of Life.

The process by which I create my dreams has often been a wild ride
on the edge of transformation. I have always been able to survive the
greatest challenges and find value in those dark passages we all pass
through. These dark passages are truly the most valuable experiences
in life because they move us beyond reasonableness and control. My

life has been more than anything I ever imagined because I've been willing to step off the edge of my reality. The extraordinary lessons of life reveal themselves to those who are willing to travel beyond what is comfortable and known.

We live in a digital age of multiple careers, genetic clones, and immediate gratification. The practice of taking a spiritual break from our daily life has become almost extinct. Rather than living spiritually we have become a culture that is spiritual on weekends, if at all. This is because our current religions have not provided an understandable and reliable spiritual guide, a map that genuinely reflects the arc of our demanding day-to-day modern lives.

In the following pages you will travel the birth/death definition we call life. You will recognize yourself at every passage because there is a master plan. Despite our unique differences, here is a clear map to follow that is common to all of us. This book alerts you to be conscious as you pass through the chaos and revelations of the thirteen rites of passage of the Circle of Life.

"These dark passages are truly the most valuable experiences in life because they move us beyond reasonableness and control."

Without a reliable spiritual map there are times when we may feel like victims of life and living. Absence of access and understanding of such a map causes us to live out the illusion that life is a struggle and, therefore, we deny our true consciousness and become saturated in half-truths and delusion. The result of this lack of awareness: 1) we remain ignorant about who we were, 2) frequently question where we are, and 3) look to others for answers to our future and by doing so we surrender our power.

With awareness of the Circle of Life we experience living as a circle filled with completions, rather than a series of incomplete cause and effect events with beginnings and ends. This profound shift in perception allows us to see completion everywhere. With awareness of the circular path, we are able to: 1) recognize and appreciate where we are from, 2) we are present where we are, and 3) consciously create where we are going.

When we see the Circle of Life as a map for living, we discover there is a design to life and we are exactly where we are supposed to be. The purpose of my life is to realize wisdom and value from my experience. Everyone experiences birth and death, puberty and midlife. We tend to experience these transforming rites of passage at around the same age. Some choose to confuse these spiritual wake-up calls for psychological problems or a major life crisis and, as a result, become victims who refuse to take responsibility for their own evolution.

Awareness of the Circle of Life helps transform the experience of crisis into an opportunity for knowledge and growth. Recognition of these opportunities empowers us to share the wisdom and value of each of the thirteen rites of passage, understanding that these are not random events but rather a spiritual map to higher consciousness. This book is about my journey, my wild ride, and what I've learned from living the Circle of Life. For context, study the rites of passage graphic and descriptions on the following pages.

The Circle of Life Passages
Frank Natale

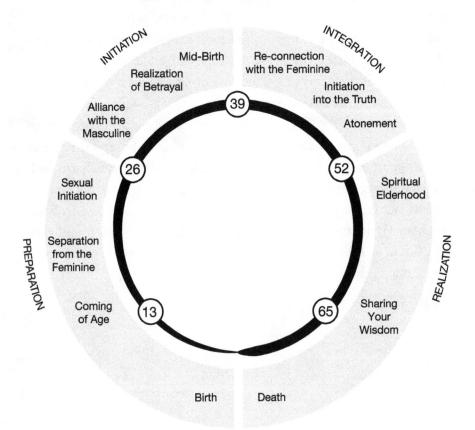

Rites of Passage

The Four Triads of Experience

PREPARATION > INITIATION > INTERGRATION > REALIZATION

The thirteen rites of passage within the Circle of Life evolve in a sequence of four triads of experiences. These triads consist of four periods of transformation.

Triad One: Preparation – Begins with passage 2 ~ Coming of Age and takes us through passage 3 ~ Separation from the Feminine and 4 ~ Sexual Initiation. This triad prepares us for living life.

Triad Two: Initiation – Begins with passage 5 ~ Alliance with the Masculine and takes us through passage 6 ~ Realization of Betrayal and 7 ~ Mid-Birth. This triad moves us beyond living life for the expectations of others and gives birth to our spiritual power.

Triad Three: Integration – Begins with passage 8 ~ Reconnection with the Feminine and takes us through passage 9 ~ Initiation into the Truth and 10 ~ Atonement. This triad prepares us for Elderhood as we return to our original nature. Integrity, honesty, forgiveness and acceptance become our priorities.

Triad Four: Realization – Begins with passage 11 ~ Spiritual Elderhood and takes us through passage 12 ~ Sharing Our New Wisdom and 13 ~ Death/Birth. This triad prepares us for the certainty of our own death and resurrection.

My Story and My Wisdom

There is a chapter devoted to each of the thirteen rites of passage and each of the chapters has two sections: "My Story" and "My Wisdom." My Story contains autobiographical notes about what I was doing and thinking while experiencing each of the passages. These are my experiences and my feelings about them. Although these passages are common to all of us, the way we transform through them is uniquely ours. My Wisdom contains my truth, insights and discoveries, which I found of value. Here I share the knowledge I've gathered from each passage. These conclusions and beliefs are based on my life experience and the shared wisdom of my teachers and mentors.

At the back of this book you will find a Self-Discovery section that provides the opportunity for you to prepare or complete each of the thirteen passages. This section describes appropriate rituals, guided visualizations and references music from my album "Rites of Passage."

The 13 Rites of Passage

There are thirteen inevitable transformations, which we all pass through in each life. When we extract wisdom and value from these thirteen rites of passage we transform and benefit from the experience rather than confuse these life-transforming events for psychological problems or emotional crisis. The wisdom realized from these passages is essential to our individual growth and the evolution of our consciousness and soul. When we live a conscious life, we are guaranteed life's most valuable reward – the transformational power of conscious experience.

1. Birth – The Gifts of Immortality and Magic
2. Coming of Age – A Time for Preparation
3. Separation from the Feminine – A Time for Separation
4. Sexual Initiation – Follow Your Passion
5. Alliance with the Masculine – The Father Quest
6. The Realization of Betrayal – The Illusion of Success
7. Mid-Birth – Birth into Our Power
8. Reconnection with the Feminine –
   Finding the Lost Pieces of Self
9. Initiation into the Truth – Letting Go of Illusions and Lies
10. Atonement – Forgiving the Sins of Sun and Moon
11. Spiritual Elderhood – Mistress and Master of Many Worlds
12. Sharing Our Wisdom – The Return Home
13. Beyond Duality – Death, the Final Passage

"Transformation is the essence of being alive.
These passages are the doorways to our power
and spiritual evolution."

Conscious or unconscious, the thirteen passages are inevitable. No one escapes them, therefore, they can be planned and anticipated rather than just experienced as an unconscious crisis we must endure and survive. Transformation is the essence of being alive. These passages are the doorways to our power and spiritual evolution. The passages within the Circle of Life are so powerful that knowing what they are and when they will come is not enough to avoid them. The only possibility we have is to accept and extract value from them while consciously experiencing them. The main passages occur approximately every thirteen years.

Coming of Age is 13 years from the first passage Birth. Alliance with the Masculine is 13 years later, around age 26. Realization of Betrayal is 3 x 13 years and begins around age 39. Reconnection with the Feminine is another 13 years at age 52. Spiritual Elderhood is attained around 65, another 13 years. Death, the Final Passage for many comes in our late 70s. Once the Circle of Life is understood we seldom confuse growth for crisis. With this knowledge, the desire and search for "who and what we are" is replaced with the satisfaction of experiencing "that we are."

Separation > Initiation > Return

Each of the thirteen passages evolves through a circular process of separation, initiation and return, a cycle of completion. Each is an adventure, beginning with leaving the comfort of our predictable reality and making the leap into the void that precedes the world of magic. "Magic" is the term I choose for the powers of manifestation available to those who consciously embrace this transformational process. The call to separate is our passion and curiosity for living. When we answer the call, we are initiated with new wisdom, powers and abilities that come to us as we encounter the challenges of each passage. Our rewards are the insights we receive from each transformational experience. We may then return and share our truth, and magic, with loved ones, colleagues and our community.

Separation

Each of us, in our own way, lives our passion and curiosity for living. Each of us separates as we leave the familiar and what we know. The desire to separate is the call of our passion. Some of us refuse the call, or compromise the opportunity, because we have been taught to fear passion, know-ing that passion has the power to transform. Most people are reluctant to transform and instead choose to live their lives in stagnation absent of magic and surprise, becoming victims of the re-fusal to change. One day I trust each of us responds to the call of our passion rather than our fears, that we realize transformation is our true spiritual work and we learn to value this as the essence of life.

Initiation

Initiation always follows separation. Initiations can be difficult, even painful. But each time we are threatened by one of life's monsters we magically draw upon resources and skills we were una-ware we possessed. These skills and magical guides only come to those who are courageous enough to transcend the comfort zone of self-imposed limitations and follow their passion.

Return

Jason, of Jason and the Argonauts, returned from his adventures with the Golden Fleece. Moses returned from the mountaintop with the Ten Commandments. Both returned home to share their truth. After enough relationships, victories and crucifixions, demons and loves, wins and losses, we all return as the Mistress and Master of many worlds. Some of us reject the call to return home because, upon return, we are refused the freedom to be our new selves. Instead, we are met with disbelief, misunderstanding and unqualified judgment. Many people are incapable of hearing your new wisdom because it threatens them.

They insist on recognizing only what they choose to see of the old you. Upon returning to his hometown Jesus was met with disbelief, even by his own mother. There he was still seen as merely the son of Joseph.

"Confusion often precedes learning something new and is an enlightened state of consciousness we have yet to recognize."

Guides for Traveling the Circle of Life

The following guides are useful reference while traveling the Circle of Life:

Guide #1: We are Still Evolving

Our evolution has only just begun so when these passages get difficult realize this may be as good as it gets for now. What we call neurosis is actually confusion that arises from having too many choices. Confusion often precedes learning something new and is an enlightened state of consciousness we have yet to recognize. Confusion creates possibilities and allows us to make choices. When we realize we are in the early stages of our evolution, neurosis is a natural and appropriate state of consciousness. When we forget this, we judge others and ourselves as if we know the criteria for a whole person. How can we know the criteria for a whole person if we ourselves are not yet whole?

We have a triune brain. Our earliest reptilian brain has taken five hundred million years to evolve into our neo cortex. This suggests our consciousness has taken as long to evolve. When we downsize this evolution to a calendar year, humans do not arrive until forty seconds before midnight on New Year's Eve. This makes most of our consciousness evolution pre-human. We are recent arrivals and therefore unqualified to judge anyone including ourselves. We don't know enough to be skeptical. At this stage in our evolution the best we can do is create a neurosis we enjoy.

"Our lives can be truly ecstatic, natural and easy when we accept that we are simply part of nature's life cycle."

Guide #2: Live and Think in Circles

"What our life is or becomes" we create, however, "How life happens" is natural like the cycles of the moon and the seasons. Our contemporary cultural models for life are linear and obsessed with physical cause-and-effect thinking. We insist every event have a reason, with a beginning, middle and an end. We mold our life in Newtonian and Cartesian thought while at the same time we know there are no facts, only agreement on particular issues. Linear thinking perpetuates negative life plans filled with disappointment and the lack of completion. Our choice to limit our lives to the linear boundaries of time and space has robbed us of our true journey. Our lives can be truly ecstatic, natural and easy when we accept that we are simply part of nature's life cycle. When we disown our miraculous evolution and deny our passion and magic, we lose the ability to experience that everything in life is moving in circles.

Life is all circles. Our days, weeks and months all move in circles. Circles large and small. Circles within circles, from the significance of our birth and death to the insignificance of leaving and returning home from work each day. Our forefathers sat in circles around fires. Egyptian mythology describes the cosmos as being round. The circle is prominent in the creation myths of cultures throughout Europe, Asia, Africa and the South Pacific. Plato described the universe as a sphere evolving within a circle. In conscious cultures, many trance dances and spiritual ceremonies begin with the formation of a sacred circle.

Etruscan soothsayers, the Egyptians, Persians and Celts worshipped the circle. Stonehenge reflects the journey of the sun through the circular year. The circular ritual of worship manifested the wheel of the Zodiac. Circular mosaic floors were used to attain altered states of consciousness in the Gothic cathedrals of Europe. Dervishes whirl in circles to transform their consciousness. North American Indians worship the Medicine Wheel and perform the circular ceremony of the Sun Dance. Alaskan Inuits slowly cut a circle in stone to initiate states of trance consciousness.

"Once we are willing to think and live our lives in circles rather than lines, we understand how the Circle of Life provides a map of our inner reality."

The Dakota Elder Black Elk said: "Everything, the power of the world, is done in a circle. The sky is round and I have heard the earth is round like a ball and so are all the stars; the wind in its greatest power whirls, birds make their nests in circles for theirs is the same religion as ours. The sun comes forth and goes down again in a circle. The moon does the same and both are round. Even the seasons form a great circle in their changing and always come back again to where they were. The life of a man is a circle from childhood to adulthood and so it is in everything where power moves."

When we think in linear terms, life and death are opposites. Life is the beginning and death is the end. What's true is that life is continuous, a circle absent a beginning and an end. Life has no opposite. There is no alternative to life. Life and death are not opposites. Birth and death are opposites. Life is a continuous flow of consciousness upon which we are born and die in infinite reincarnations. Experiencing life as circular does not require a great deal of spiritual work because its presence is visible everywhere. Once we are willing to think and live our lives in circles rather than lines, we understand how the Circle of Life provides a map of our inner reality. This map guides our soul in its spiritual development and supports those who choose to move on to greater states of awareness. When we experience life as a circle, we are complete. We discover there is a map to life and we are exactly where we are supposed to be.

"Change is superficial. Transformation is deep. Transformation alters our perception of reality and therefore causes everything in our life to change. Transformation is what happens when we live our life rather than analyze it."

Guide #3: Think Transformation Rather than Change

To transform and receive value from each passage we must appreciate the differences between transformation and change. Transformation is the willingness to have an experience beyond form. It is the capacity to value space, the potential for form and what has yet to be revealed. What is most valuable about a car is the space inside its form that allows us to get in and go. What is valuable about a glass is the space inside the glass that creates choices like drinking water or holding flowers. What is precious within all form is the emptiness that yields space for our creativity and experience. What is valuable in our relationships is the space to transform. When such space is recognized our relationships are complete and we create new space and new relationships.

Everything, and everyone, transforms. This is the nature of the universe. Wood in fire transforms to heat and gas. Likewise, we transform when we travel through the fire of significant life passages as our current point of view transforms into an entirely new experience of life. Transformation is beyond simple change. Change is painting the facade of our house without fixing the rotten plumbing and faulty electricity. Change is waking up one morning and realizing we married our father or mother (again). Change only provides a temporary high, an illusion of wellbeing. Change is superficial. Transformation is deep. Transformation alters our perception of reality and therefore causes everything in our life to change. Transformation is what happens when we live our life rather than analyze it. Transformation often requires mixed emotions, confusion, physical change and the risk of inspiration. Transformation causes thoughts, beliefs and behavior to transform at their roots, which is why we resist it so. Transformation is the only reliable indicator of a consciously evolving human being.

Chart of Transformational Experience
Frank Natale

Being Present
(Experience and Awareness of that Experience)

Being Responsible for Your Life

Being Conscious and Aware of Your Life

Accepting that Transformation is Continuous in Your Life

Mid-Birth: The Threshold of Transformation
Discontent / Fear of Worsening / Doubt

Temporary High / Illusion of Well-Being

The Cycle of Change

Looking for Someone or Something to Save Us

Being Stuck in Form, Beliefs and Points of View

Being Unpleasantly at the Effect of Life

The Chart of Transformational Experience shows the upward movement of our consciousness, which liberates us from being stuck in form and allows us to accept transformation. Many people unconsciously live the majority of their life going round and round in the cycle of change, being at the effect of life, and the fear of worsening that exists below the threshold of transformation. The reason so many of us get stuck in form, and are unpleasantly at the effect of life, is we live within belief systems, which we ourselves did not consciously create.

When stuck in form we hurry to change things rather than allowing them time to transform. The result is we confuse change for growth and then realize, often too late, only the form has changed not the way we live and perceive our life. Two essential ingredients must occur simultaneously for transformation to happen: We must be willing to risk having a new experience and be cognitive about that experience. Neither cognition nor experience alone will engender transformation. You must be both willing and aware.

Guide #4: The 5 Phases of Transformation

All transformation has the same basic structure, which promotes and sustains the process. The way we transform is up to us, however, the procedure and structure is always the same. Throughout all the phases, remember life is the destruction and re-creation of self and what we see at any given moment is only a piece of our whole self. I have also suggested some rituals to help you identify the phase of transformation you are experiencing now. What is important about a ritual is what we believe we are doing, not what we are actually doing.

Phase #1: Letting Go – This phase consists of making a conscious choice to let go of an old way of being. In this initial phase we determine what we are willing to let go of and review our resources and rank our status in life. We all have difficulty letting go of familiar circumstances, even when they are unhealthy. We trust these worn-out beliefs that once worked for us. In order to grow, to move on, we must demonstrate the courage to let go. Use of rituals and symbols will help this process. Create an object made of possessions symbolizing what or whom you are willing to let go. With reverence and clear intention, bury the object in the ground, release it into the wind, throw it into water or burn it in a ritual fire. Let it go.

Phase #2: The Void – This phase is a wandering period, a time of confusion, when we have no vision of the future. The void is a sacred gap absent of thought. The void is an emptiness that has been a part of all of our significant life passages. This is the phase of transformation we resist the most because it makes us fearful and uncertain. We experience no progress, only loss. The mistake is to insist on moving quickly beyond the void. Being confused is part of the process. As we walk through this "time between dreams" confusion simply means we are about to learn something of great value and importance. Crisis is the potential for opportunity. An empty cup or bowl symbolizes this phase. A receptive ritual may include sitting quietly with open hands turned toward the sky. Close your eyes, breathe deeply and allow your cognitive structure to dissolve. Be open to the possibilities.

Phase #3: Conflict – The third phase is filled with polar opposites and clashing emotions, which cause frustration as we are pulled in several directions at once. One of the gifts of transformation is to reconcile these conflicts. It is wise to exercise patience and allow these conflicting values to reveal themselves rather than hurry or force a choice between one and the other. Awareness of these questions and doubts eventually transform the conflict and inspire creativity. Consider contrasting symbols such as lemons and chocolate, sunlight and darkness, winter and summer, feathers and stones. Embrace the textures, meaning and values of each.

Phase #4: Vision – The period of chaos subsides and manifests a

new point of view, which empowers us to see a new life, a fresh beginning and ultimately a new way of living and relating to the world
around us. Appropriate symbols and rituals for this phase include birth,
eggs, sowing of seeds, a vision quest, the planting of trees and flowers,
lighting candles, writing a letter expressing gratitude to a teacher or
loved one.

Phase #5: Manifesting – The final phase occurs when we surround
ourselves with results, affirming we have chosen a new direction. To
accomplish this, we must make a firm and clear commitment to our
future, trusting we will conquer all distractions. Sometimes the result
may take longer than we are willing to wait. In these moments it is
best to be patient and look for new opportunities. Accept and honor the
results in your life, create visual and audible affirmations of what you
are willing to have and be, acknowledge yourself and others that support your new direction. Be present and actualize new opportunities. Be
clear. Enjoy yourself.

*"Rituals are healthy routines we create
in order to stay centered during difficult times.
They are powerful catalysts driving us to new
visions and the realization of higher values."*

Guide #5: The Value of Ritual

The power of rituals is that they reveal understanding beyond rational
linear thinking. We are able to grasp deeper and larger visions that to
the logical mind seem hopelessly complex or contradictory. Ritual has
the power to move us beyond our struggle to a new level of understanding so we may truly embrace the incomprehensible. When we allow
this new level of understanding to manifest, we experience the freedom
and flight of dancing into ecstatic states or the solitude of a vision quest
that speaks to our whole being. Ritual helps us to maintain our strength

during the initial chaos of significant transformational passages. Ritual gives us the courage to be present and accept the experience rather than sink into a state of denial. When we maintain strong and clear intentions, ritual allows us to see there is more to life than the current passage. Rituals are healthy routines we create in order to stay centered during difficult times. They are powerful catalysts driving us to new visions and the realization of higher values.

When we start living our new vision the role of ritual takes on a new importance. In our new vision ritual serves to center us during times of crisis and also initiates and promotes growth. Without ritual our rites of passage can be empty experiences of crisis we have only survived. Profound life passages come with periods of inertia. This upsets us because our culture is ruled by logic and we expect continuous movement through difficult times in an orderly manner. Ritual promotes intent and generates inspiration. It allows us to experience spiritual inspiration absent of the egotistical interpretations of earthly cultural authority. Ritual is the context for spiritual experience.

Passage 1 ~ Birth

The Gifts of Immortality and Magic

My Story About Magic and Birth

What I know about my birth is based on the gossip of my ancestors. I studied with Bucky Fuller and was re-birthed by Sondra Ray. I've done Psychodrama with Jacob Moreno and Lou Yablonsky, been Rolfed, encountered by Fritz Perls and Carl Rogers and actualized with Abe Maslow. I've stood on my head chanting "Om Namah Shivaya" with Baba Muktananda, shaved my head and bent my body like a pretzel with Swami Satchidananda. I trained with Werner Erhard, fasted with Gabriel Cousens, and participated in Ayahuasca rituals deep in the Amazon. I've channeled the Mayans at Tulum and Tikal, and trance danced with the Sangoma of South Africa and the Santo Daime of Brazil. I've done all of this and I am still unable to recall the experience of my birth. I have many recalls of life experience in pre-human forms, but as a human being I have no direct recollection. While doing evolution recall work, I remember thinking maybe this is my first life as a human being.

I have plenty of family gossip. I was a war baby born in 1941. The term "war baby" was used so often I thought I was trouble and may have been responsible for World War II. Although born on June 22, 1941, as an adult, I preferred to drum from sundown the night of June 21 through to sunrise the morning of June 22, the longest day and shortest night of the year. I celebrated my magic and immortality by throwing a ritual party called the "Festival of Light" each year. Some of the most magical of these parties have been celebrated at my home on the Spanish island of Ibiza.

I was born into an extended Italian family that lived in connected brownstones in Bedford-Stuyvesant, Brooklyn, close to Ebbets Field. I have no conscious memories until I was around three or four years old. There were three families with children, my sickly aunt and my single aunt and uncle. The family was run under the tight control of my matriarch grandmother. New York was very segregated in those days with the Irish-Americans one block to the north and the African-Americans one block to the south. It was a time when kids played on the street and doors were left unlocked. I belonged and felt secure.

Our small area provided a world of adventure. I played under the kitchen table while my mother and aunts cooked. I jumped the back roofs and climbed the fences, played games with cousins and friends. I witnessed older kids fight violent gang wars and learned to survive the daily trips back and forth to school. I learned how to swear from my Uncle Joe who was always busy shining his shoes or his Mercury convertible. I seldom traveled alone beyond the boundaries of the block because it was considered dangerous.

We had huge Christmas feasts where we were required to perform theatrical skits. Family and guests enjoyed my dancing the most. They would roll back the rug and I dazzled them with my footwork. I enjoyed dressing-up in army, cowboy and baseball uniforms and having my picture taken. Although a shy child, I would do almost anything for attention.

I didn't realize I was handicapped until later in life. My father refused to accept that he had a son born with congenital cataracts and diagnosed industrially blind. As a result, my father and I spent a lot of time in hospital eye clinics searching for a cure. These clinics always smelled of chemicals and echoed with the moans of suffering patients. I enjoyed my magical, slightly out of focus view of the world and resented wasting free time with doctors shining lights in my eyes.

As a small child, I spent hours playing with my friends outside

Ebbets Field waiting for a chance to catch a baseball the Brooklyn Dodgers hit out of the park. I couldn't play baseball because I couldn't see the ball. I couldn't play football or basketball because I was too small. I was the kid nobody wanted on their team, unless they were desperate or needed an umpire. I remember laughing at this thinking, "I'm a blind umpire." After much humiliation I rejected interest in sports and spent my time drawing, painting, playing drums, dancing and listening to music.

"The birth of our immortality is not about this life or past lives. The ancestry of our immortality dates back to our earliest evolution."

My Wisdom About Magic and Birth

At birth we are welcomed back to the material world of magic and wonder. Birth and death are time distinctions and exist as our thoughts. They exist within our physical world and are not absolutes. Life is absolute and has no opposite. When I say, "There is no alternative to life." I mean it literally. Life is continuous, without beginning or end. Life is an endless circle within which we consciously, or unconsciously, choose birth and death.

Much of our behavior has been learned and passed down from our animal ancestors. Our courtship rituals, our sexual performance, dancing, speech, hunting and other survival behavior all came from our ability to observe and copy animals. Our early ancestors knew they had evolved from other animals. They saw and felt the similarities between themselves and other life forms. It was instinctive and natural. Belief and scientific data were not required.

Knowledge of our animal ancestors has been lost. The Indo-European invasions of peaceful agricultural communities, Ice Ages, The Inquisition, Witch Hunts, The Crusades all contribute to why Western Europeans and their descendants have forgotten their animal origins.

Our shamanic roots were destroyed. Our spiritual ancestors were persecuted and eliminated from "history" books. Shamanism in other parts of the world went unpunished and was allowed to evolve into various religions, most notably Indian Hinduism, which recognized, in symbol and ritual, the value of our origins. The birth of our immortality is not about this life or past lives. The ancestry of our immortality dates back to our earliest evolution. With focused intent and ritual, we may recall lives in other than human form.

In my early twenties I suspected I had lived before in pre-human form and chose to re-experience those births. I began working with evolutionary recall and recorded a continuous Om sound that replicates the vibration of source. Over this Om sound I superimposed the rhythm of a human heartbeat that varied from slow to fast and then dropped to very slow and then to still. This repeated rhythmic cycle helped me access an altered trance state and experience sequential births, lives and deaths. I was astonished as I recalled a succession of lives and deaths ranging from sea life to apes.

As I recalled this evolution major behavior patterns fell away effortlessly. Our present life is transformed by recalling pre-human lives and deaths. I had loved to sunbathe. During evolutionary recall I was a simple sea form absent of will being tossed about by ocean currents. The tide washed me onto the shore and left me to bake to death in the sun. After that recall I lost all desire to tan in the sun.

Our grounding in logic and science requires tangible evidence to believe we are immortal. We are shown the overwhelming scientific proof contained within our own bodies yet we continue to deny we have evolved from pre-human life forms. To avoid our pre-human ancestry, we create spiritual terms like Kundalini to explain natural occurrence rather than admit we have a tailbone that once had a tail. Small bumps appear when our skin is exposed to the cold. These are the remnants of muscles that once raised hairs covering our entire body that served to trap atmospheric air close to our body and helped to keep us warm.

We remove our appendix, once an integral part of our digestive system that functioned to digest the raw grass and leaves that were over 90% of our diet. We now cook our food, which kills its energy and forces our body to use its own depleted energy and digestive resources.

Absent of the need to kill our prey, the canine teeth are long gone. Our wisdom teeth are expendable, as we no longer need them to mash roots and crush nuts, and many children today are born without them.

Our human DNA is 97.6% the same as a chimpanzee. In time we will be viewed no different from this ape than a zebra is different from a horse. It is our intelligence, not our bodies that will prove to be very different.

The bone structure of our hands is the same as a dolphin fin. Whales and dolphins left the sea eighty million years ago and returned to the sea sixty million years ago. These sea mammals are our relatives.

The small pink triangle in the corner of our eyes is what remains of a horizontal eyelid that moved across the eyes to protect us from the elements. We still have the muscles to move our ears, which was essential to our survival when hearing was a dominant sense. With the domination of eyesight, these once indispensable muscles have been rendered useless.

The most astonishing evidence of our immortality is our reptilian triune brain. This is the oldest part of our brain, evolving over five hundred million years, and is tenaciously responsible for the essentials of our survival. The primitive brain regulates instinctive behavior and vital biological functions and rhythms, controlling our breath and body temperature, critical responsibilities the wisdom of nature did not delegate to our emotional midbrain or our inconsistent neo-cortex.

The mammalian or limbic midbrain is three hundred million years old and is the center of our emotions, memory, attention and learning. The limbic brain system transforms objective sensory input and reason into subjective human experience and, therefore, profoundly influences our relationships and abilities to function in society.

The neo-cortex is our newest mammalian brain, which is two hundred million years old and the source of reasoning and, in humans, language. This part of the brain empowers us to communicate, understand, empathize, and experience compassion and love.

> *"We continue to evolve faster than any other life form and have chosen to evolve beyond the limited perceptions of fate and destiny. We are the consciousness who determines the value of all other matter in our reality."*

There is a fourth brain, the cerebellum, thought to be growing ten times faster than other parts of the brain. Unlike the other components, the cells of the cerebellum are arranged in a precise fashion similar to a computer. This unique cellular group functions to inhibit or restrain, which provides for the immediate and continuous monitoring and adjustment of actions initiated by the cerebral cortex.

It's difficult to see why we deny our immortality when faced with evidence that we are walking around with a five hundred-million-year-old brain and a body that is a testimony to our immortality. We continue to evolve faster than any other life form and have chosen to evolve beyond the limited perceptions of fate and destiny. We are the consciousness who determines the value of all other matter in our reality. Ultimately, we determine which flowers and animals will survive and those that will become extinct. We have evolved to the point where this responsibility is ours, not nature.

We are very powerful, far more powerful than we have been taught or are willing to acknowledge. We are immortal and have decided the best way to predict the future is to create it. There is no precedent for us. With the evolution of each new brain, we become more sophisticated communicators. This expanded consciousness has evolved so rapidly we are more often confused and frustrated by this greater awareness than enlightened or excited by its enormous power and possibility.

What our culture tends to call neurotic is really our ability to see things from more than one point of view. This is not a problem. This is what has empowered us as creators who make conscious choices. Consider how we perceive our relationships. When we look at a relationship through our primitive reptilian brain, it can cause us to become jealous enough to leave that relationship. Our mammalian brain wants to stay in the relationship and to belong, even become married and have children. Our neo-cortex is willing to throw it all away for a career. We consider the possible sacrifice of love and relationship for promotion and notoriety.

This new multi-layered perception has lifted us beyond fate to the freedom of choice, the choice to do one or more or all of the above. We are empowered with this freedom because we are capable of seeing the same reality from different points of view. Before development of the neo-cortex, we were victims and unaware of our choices.

Our bodies are a living testament to our immortality demonstrated whenever we observe a fetus gestating in the womb or an infant struggling to walk. In the womb, the fetus evolves through multiple stages beginning with the physical form of a fish and into the form of an ape. Early in this microcosm of evolution, we observe gills appearing on the sides of the fish-shaped head. We observe movement through various physical transformations ending with an ape-like form. Birth follows, which is a reenactment of our prehistoric transformation from being a life form that is water dependent to one that breathes air.

"Birth is also a gift of magic. From birth to around seven years old we witness with wonder the magic of the physical world. Our magical consciousness continues until we sacrifice our magic for understanding."

The movement of an infant as they struggle to walk demonstrates the prehistoric evolution of our consciousness. Walking cannot be taught. We can only support the infant to recall this behavior from their evolutionary memory. Consider the evolution of these six movements that we have all observed.

Fish Movement – The first of the movements is when the infant lies on their belly rocking side to side with little independent movement of the head from the body. Often the legs and arms are up and extended, the entire position simulating a fish.

Amphibian Movement – Next is the movement of the upper part of the body, the arms and hands pulling the infant in a forward movement without any help or support from the legs and lower part of the body. This is amphibious and represents when we moved from our origins in the prehistoric seas to the land.

Reptilian Movement – The lower limbs quickly move into action coordinated with the upper part of the body. This rapid synchronized movement propels the infant forward reflecting the scurry of a reptile.

Mammalian Movement – The infant belly lifts off the ground, the child begins to move about on all fours in the same fashion as the next evolutionary step of the small mammal.

Ape Movement – With minor support to maintain balance, the infant stands, takes its first step and, in ape-like fashion, sways side to side as it cautiously moves forward.

Human Movement – Finally, the sixth movement brings us into present time when the child walks, runs and stands erect as Homo sapiens.

Given all the physical evidence, it should be easy to accept our evolution and immortality and therefore receive our birth as our gift of immortality. Birth is also a gift of magic. From birth to around seven years old we witness with wonder the magic of the physical world. Our magical consciousness continues until we sacrifice our magic for understanding. This core of magic remains buried deep beneath the layers of our conditioned maturity.

This magical period reflects the time when we were not yet fully present in the physical world. Our body was birthed, but our conscious perceptions were not. Our belief systems had not had time to form, so we remained open to experience. As children we lived in the moment and everything was alive. We communicated with plants, animals, and objects and perceived consciousness in everything. We easily became distracted and drifted into altered states having conversations with bodiless entities no one else could hear or see.

Why most of us don't remember much of the first five to seven years of our life is because we weren't present much of the time. We try to remember this period, but the criteria we use deceives us by causing us to look for recognizable childhood events rather than the pure joy of magical conscious experience.

I recognize the magic of my early childhood and the magic that has also appeared throughout my adult life. While visiting the Guatemalan rainforest I was invited to a sunset ritual with the Indians living on Lake Peten Itza. With great expectation I envisioned fire torches and Indians wearing feathers, but instead the people arrived in soiled Western clothing, with dogs barking and babies howling, everyone talking and laughing as they waded into the lake until the water was up to their necks.

My hosts invited me to join them in the water. I politely refused after sighting crocodiles floating nearby with eyes gazing out over the lake. The village people laughed at me saying, "We would not come in with our children if it was not safe." I remained on the shore and before long the sun sank low behind the trees on the opposite side of the lake. Everyone, with heads barely above the water, became completely still. The dogs and babies fell silent. The ripples on the surface of the lake vanished and, as the sun set, the lake became a mirror reflecting the rich pastel colors of the sky above.

In that moment, to my amazement, I spontaneously slid into the water like a snake without making a ripple. I discovered why the people encouraged me to come into the water. I held my head motionless and, like everyone else, maintained an angle that removed the far shoreline. All the land vanished and my entire view was filled with the magnificent magenta colors from the heavens above and the mirrored reflection on the lake below. In a state of wonder, I gazed silently out at the magic of the lake and the sky, humbly connected to everything and everyone, even the nearby crocodiles. We were all hypnotized, transformed into a collective magical trance. Once darkness came, everyone rushed out of the water and celebrated the experience by lighting fires, eating, talking and singing songs.

> *"Once we realize that magic is the norm and not the exception, magic is everywhere and we are able to reclaim the powerful perceptions of our childhood."*

We tend to search for magic as if magic is odd and unusual, rather than simply allowing the magic of experience to become part of our reality. We travel to extraordinary sacred places and the incredible power places nature has provided. We worship and wonder. We alter our reality with teacher plants, which empower us to fly the inner landscape of our minds. We seek gurus and masters who will recognize us. Some even suffer starvation, isolation, and body mutilation in search of spiritual experience. Book after book and fast after fast, the quest for magical experience continues with almost obsessive zeal as if magic will appear like a rabbit from a hat.

Once we realize that magic is the norm and not the exception, magic is everywhere and we are able to reclaim the powerful perceptions of our childhood. We can stop condemning magic with our denial of its existence. We can stop murdering magic with our need for understanding. Instead, we may respect and welcome magic as an integral part of our lives.

Magic is everywhere. Beyond nature, magic is also inherent in our science and technology. Magic is not only natural it is unnatural.

Whether it is a water lily opening and closing to the passing sun or a television allowing us to tune in as many realities as we have channels and time to experience. All of it is magic.

Magic is genius. During their magical early years, children are far more intelligent than after they have been taught the inhibition of adulthood. As children we mastered arts and science at speeds faster than our cluttered adult mind will allow. As children many had to be a genius to survive parenting and other inadequate paths that lead toward self-reliance. Genius is to know something without ever having experienced it. Genius is magic and the source is our immortality. Our magic returns with each birth.

PREPARATION (13 to 26 Years)

Passage 2 ~ Coming of Age

A Time for Preparation

The First Triad: Preparation

Coming of Age begins the First Triad: Preparation, which also includes Passage 3 ~ Separation from the Feminine and Passage 4 ~ Sexual Initiation. These passages serve to prepare us for our Father Quest as we enter the world of the masculine.

> *"My life has been a series of little deaths and births. Whenever I found myself buried in the negativity of my surroundings a voice inside would say, 'There is more to life than this.' I would move on and be reborn."*

My Story About Coming of Age

As a young person, I was very curious and adventurous and, as a result, I was always in trouble. In school I was sent to the dean's office and punished when I refused to allow my fine arts teacher to paint over my paintings. I smoked grass at a time when authorities believed marijuana led to heroin. I drove my father's car without permission and tore the porch off the side of our house. I was punished for playing seductive games with my cousins. Eventually, I became rebellious and willing to pay for the consequences of my actions.

As an adult, I know an artist should never paint over another person's work and smoking grass does not lead to anything but great sex and uncontrollable laughter. I know now, as a young person, I was too alive and too willing to explore. Coming of age was a thrilling, but rough time for me. I got in trouble with one authority after another. In order to survive street gangs in 1950s Brooklyn I adapted to my environment. I began to think negatively and modeled the actions of the neighborhood Mafia types. In my world violence and prejudice were ways of life. I began to identify with losers. My early life was neatly wrapped in a Christian-Judaic morality that only further crippled me. My creativity always helped me to survive. I always assimilated and adapted and still do. My life has been a series of little deaths and births. Whenever I found myself buried in the negativity of my surroundings a voice inside would say, "There is more to life than this." I would move on and be reborn.

A large portion of the pier in Manhattan Beach was being torn down. I dared three friends to climb aboard a section of the pier and use it as a raft. We jumped on and, without considering the consequences, I cut the rope and we drifted away from shore. We attempted to use boards as oars, but the raft was too large to control. Desperate, I jumped into the water but it was so cold I couldn't move. A friend extended a piece of wood and saved me from drowning. Wet and freezing, we huddled close until a police helicopter finally spotted us and called the Coast Guard. We were rescued. A little further and we would have been swept out to sea. I got home wet, cold and very late for dinner. I was excited about my adventure and eager to tell my mother about what had happened. Before I could speak, she started beating me with a broom for being late for dinner. The next day everyone knew because the story was published in the *New York Daily News*. Despite my fame and good fortune my parents grounded me for weeks.

When I was 13 my father informed my sister and I we were moving from our extended Italian family parente home in Bed-Stuy to a middle-class neighborhood in Coney Island. I sat in our new home in shock telling my sister, "This is it? Where is everybody?" Suddenly, there were no more friends or cousins to play with. The old neighborhood was gone. It was just my mother, father, sister and me. In this new environment, absent the relatives, for the first time I realized and accepted who my parents were. There were no more choices, only the two of them, my mother and father. That's when I began to fantasize about leaving home.

One summer day I was on the subway going to my first job in a box factory. It was hot and the train was filled with people going to Coney Island amusement park and the beach. Not me. I was on the train going to a job my father had arranged to teach me the value of work. Within a month I vowed, "I will never have a real job again." And I never have. I remember thinking that making boxes is really boring and if I got promoted, I will supervise people making boxes. I quit. Disappointed, my father saw my choice as rebellion. He put me into St. Simon & Jude Catholic School where I was required to wear a red, white and blue uniform every day. I remember the nuns wore long black veils and swaying crucifixes. The nuns were mean, would hit us with rulers and make us kneel for hours saying prayers on hard wooden pews.

My father was obsessed with having my vision corrected so I could compete in sports and school. He insisted I have an operation on my eyes. He insisted I be brave and read about the operation including how they would pop my eye from its socket during the course of the surgery. I lay in the operating room terrified, with only local anesthesia, watching the scalpel moving toward my eye. Then all I saw was blood. I was in a state of shock while they operated, thinking it would all be over soon. The recovery was worse than the surgery. I was drugged to ease the constant pain in a hospital ward filled with men sixty years and older. Recovery required another two months at home with both eyes covered and my arms strapped to my bed to prevent me from touching my eyes, which were in continuous pain. After all my pain and suffering the operation was a failure and did not improve my vision at all.

In our home physical violence was a regular occurrence. My father was an amateur boxer and his hands were quick to strike. Many friends have shared they learned to be in present time by studying meditation with an Eastern master. I learned to be in present time in a boxing ring.

If you are not present in the ring you go unconscious. My father's violence made me the referee again, only this time to protect my mother and sister. The violence at home left deep wounds in all of us. Many years later I went to see Robert De Niro in *Raging Bull*, a film about the boxer Jake La Motta. When the family violence scenes began, I became nauseous and ran out of the movie.

Our family meals were also a war zone. Conversations always ending in confrontation. I discovered early on, it was best to shut up and eat. When the dinner table arguments stopped, the racial jokes would start. I became ashamed of my family and stopped bringing friends home. I began to withdraw. At fifteen I met Ronnie, a Sephardic Jew from another neighborhood and an outsider. My family cautioned me about Ronnie, but we became fast friends. He turned me on to drums, modern jazz, Greenwich Village, LSD and smoking grass. We'd spend hours listening to music and playing drums in his basement or getting stoned and laughing until our bellies hurt and we fell to the floor. There was no rock and roll yet, only Pat Boone and Black gospel music. We would go to Greenwich Village to hear Miles Davis, Chet Baker and Art Blakey. This was the beginning of an exciting new adventure. Eventually I would leave home and live a bohemian nomadic lifestyle that lasted forty years. I did not leave home because I was bored and lusted for life. I left home because there was more pain and judgment there than I could handle.

In those days LSD was legal. We would do outrageous things like go to the Brooklyn Zoo or ride the Cyclone and Thunderbolt roller coasters at Coney Island. Once I was arrested for dancing with a mannequin in Macy's department store. The police had no knowledge of LSD. They thought I was crazy and locked me up until the police psychiatrist could evaluate me the next morning. After answering inane questions, the psychiatrist informed the arresting officer they would have to release me. The officer went wild, "He is crazy. He was crazy."

To earn money, I delivered shoeboxes filled with numbers for the local bookies. Other neighborhood teens were hired to stage street fights to divert the police while local criminals committed larger crimes. The butcher shop, bakery and Italian restaurant were fronts for the local bookies and gamblers. Only the neighborhood people knew the restaurant had no kitchen. Its menu listed specialties from nearby restaurants and cafés. When food was ordered it was called in and quickly picked up from these other neighborhood restaurants, reheated, plated and served. Family friends were always stopping by to sell clothes and electronic equipment that had recently "fallen off the back of a truck." I remember thinking there was more crime in this middle-class neighborhood than in the ghetto of Bed-Stuy, Brooklyn.

"Growing up as a teenager in New York had many rites of passage. We challenged each other by jumping the roofs of buildings, we'd run and leap from one roof to the other without looking down."

One day I was standing on the corner with my friends when I looked across the street and saw my father standing on the opposite corner with his cronies. I was clear then that I would find a way out of this neighborhood. Within a week my wish came true. I had given some grass to a friend whose father caught him smoking. The next day his father had me beaten by local tough guys who warned me to stay out of the neighborhood. I left that world and started hanging out in other neighborhoods. My father was plainly hurt. He thought I had abandoned him. I never told him how the people he admired had beaten me and threatened to kill me because I smoked pot and refused their invitation to become a thief.

Growing up as a teenager in New York had many rites of passage. We challenged each other by jumping the roofs of buildings, we'd run and leap from one roof to the other without looking down. Another time I had to wear woman's hair rollers and walk in Central Park accepting all the ensuing harassment. During such stunts there were always a few guys watching to help if I got beaten. Even though I was small and almost blind I was accepted in the group because I was courageous. I wasn't tough enough or big enough to be of any help in the regular weekend gang fights, but my humor and talent for verbal jousting was immediately appreciated and put to use. In time I became known by nicknames such as Magoo, Tongue Fu and The Mouth.

I was the gang jester with a lot of pull with gang leadership much like medieval court jesters influenced the king. I was the guy who was funny and entertained, the lead man who went into another gang's territory and jokes, humiliates and insults the opponents before the actual fight starts. I was respected for my verbal skills and had made it within my world. I was finally good enough. Later in life, as a therapist and encounter master, I became known for creating a style of compassionate confrontation called "kissed by lightning."

I was shy with girls but befriended them easily. One night nine of us piled into an old Chevy and went to the movies. My friend Little Joe was unable to go and asked me to watch out for his girlfriend. The car was so crowded Joe's girl asked to sit on my lap and we teased each other, which was as far as sex usually went in the 50s. The next day as I entered Jimmy's Candy Store, our local hang out, without warning Little Joe punched me in the face and accused me of coming on to his girlfriend. We did not speak for months. A mutual friend later told me Little Joe had overdosed. I was shocked and saddened and swore never to flirt with a friend's girlfriend again.

> *"I loved New York City. When I turned seventeen, I moved, never to return to Brooklyn other than to visit family. I settled in Greenwich Village, entered art school and became a hippie."*

I began to spend less time in Brooklyn, preferring to cross the Brooklyn Bridge into Manhattan where I discovered new friends and challenges. I danced at The New York Palladium three times a week where I was called The Kid. There I met Ida and Tito Puente, danced on Lionel Hampton's drums and snorted cocaine with Count Basie. I loved New York City. When I turned seventeen, I moved, never to return to Brooklyn other than to visit family. I settled in Greenwich Village, entered art school and became a hippie. Dressed in black, with long dark hair, full beard and sunglasses, all you could see was a pink nose coming down the street. Poor eyesight and shyness added to my mysterious image. I studied interior design and fine arts. The interior design work was difficult because of my poor eyesight, but I excelled at fine arts, which poured out of me naturally. I soon discovered a form of Benzedrine that dilated my pupils giving me the eyesight the doctors had promised but failed to deliver. Speed and marijuana became my way of self-medicating.

Painting and sculpture became the media for my anger and rebelliousness. My work was good enough the arty crowd at school embraced me as a serious artist. It was during this period I got to know the movers and shakers of the New York art scene, people like Andy Warhol and Henry Geldzahler. My friends and I would hang out until all hours at Max's Kansas City and Oleg Cassini's Tenement. Arty parties and smoking grass made school impossible. After two years I left college to become an artist. Ultimately, the New York art scene was too shallow for me. I felt out of place and incapable of participating in the backbiting and catty talk that monopolized every conversation. At dinner parties I was "the onion in the room" continuously being asked what it was like to have been a rebellious Brooklyn street kid who was now part of the sophisticated New York art scene. I was never comfortable being the kid from the Brooklyn ghetto in a room full of shallow and snobby odd balls.

After two years of hobnobbing in the flighty New York art scene I followed a girl friend to San Diego where she had joined Synanon to heal her drug problem. Our plan was to leave Synanon when she felt ready and live in Mexico. When she was ready to go, however, I was not. The revolutionary spirit and flamboyant personality of Synanon founder Chuck Dederich would keep me there for almost four years.

"I had found another place where I belonged. Here my teachers and friends were just as rebellious as I was, but they expressed their discontent constructively."

Friends in New York couldn't believe I chose to be in San Diego. For them this was a small, uncultured Navy town. Some friends accused Synanon of holding me against my will. For me it was home. I had found another place where I belonged. Here my teachers and friends were just as rebellious as I was, but they expressed their discontent constructively. Chuck and his peers hammered on my rock, opening the rebellious young man from Brooklyn to philosophy, politics and psychology.

Unable to control my longing for adventure, I volunteered to open a Synanon artist commune in San Francisco. There I continued painting and sculpture work with fellow artists and musicians like Charlie Haden and Joe Pass. Everything, even food and sleep, took a low priority to our art. This was an exciting time and I became a prolific artist. Then I chose to join the Synanon Dirty Dozen, a team of twelve men who moved to Reno, Nevada and went into Nevada State Prison in Carson City every day to work with the inmates.

I was terrified the first day I entered the prison. Huge muscle-bound men filled the maximum-security recreation yard. On sight they yelled "fresh meat" and threatened to rape me. Everything from thieves to murderers, these were the same men with whom I would conduct encounter sessions. I was scared at first, but my ability to play Brooklyn tough guy, along with my sense of humor and experience as the gang jester, allowed me to say things these guys normally would kill someone for saying. The prison was hardcore. Drug use was common and murder occurred weekly, usually over gambling debts. It was legal to gamble because the prison was located in Nevada.

One of my assignments was to work with inmates on death row, the ones waiting to be executed. I found myself locked in their world, a six by ten-foot space, where they moved like caged animals. I learned to have conversations mirroring their movements. I met men doing ten to life for murder and others, amazingly, doing long sentences for possessing marijuana. Eventually we received permission to start our own separate commune within maximum-security. In one encounter group one inmate was verbally attacking another. The inmate being attacked was a very large man who begged me to get the other guy to back off, but I hesitated. In frustration the large man stood and ripped the bolted chair out of the floor and threatened to kill the other inmate. I stood between them and was able to make them stop. The large man later thanked me for stopping him as he pulled back his jacket and flashed a homemade gun. In that moment I realized the danger. Before that I was just a kid from Brooklyn playing tough guy.

In time we opened a similar community within minimum security and were given permission to establish the Peavine Honor Camp, a string of long-house dormitories out in the desert with no walls, only a barbed wire fence. It held thirty-five inmates doing life without the possibility of parole and one correction officer who had little to do but play cards with the inmates. We would spend hours each day, seven days a week encountering each other's pretense and defensive blocks. These men became the best encounter masters I ever trained. For the years we ran the honor camp there was never an escape attempt or a violent episode. A new administration closed the camp and cancelled our contract. The greatest injustice was they returned the inmates we worked with into the general population where they were beaten because they had joined us.

Then Chuck Dederich asked me to come to Los Angeles to do public relations. Hollywood had embraced Synanon and the Synanon group lived in a large house on the beach near Santa Monica Pier. A new life became filled with movie stars, sunshine, and glorious sunsets. I was far away from the crime and violence of New York and I liked it. The only thing about California that reminded me of New York was the crazy street people who paraded down the beach in front of our house.

One afternoon I was taking a break sitting on the promenade when I saw an older man with long gray hair walking a Russian wolfhound that looked just like him. To my surprise he walked right up to me and said, "Hello, my name is Michael. I was your mother in a past life and I'm here to guide you." Being from Brooklyn I assumed he was trying to get into my pants.

Despite my initial paranoia, Michael turned out to be straight and practically adopted me as his son and apprentice. Michael introduced me to the occult and his spiritual principles of unconditional love, communications and self-awareness. I attended séances where he spoke in tongues, materialized ghosts and healed the sick. I was totally transformed and became his grateful student for over a year. One day without warning Michael told me he would be leaving and within days he literally disappeared. At that time there was no popular New Age movement, but years later Michael would be channeled and have books written about "The Michael Teachings."

"In our culture we take longer than any other life form to leave the nest. There is a resistance, almost a fear of going out into the world of adventure because there is little clarity about whether we are prepared enough."

My Wisdom About Coming of Age

The thirteen years that precede the Coming of Age passage are about nurturing, which takes place in the home, the domain of the mother. At Coming of Age, we begin to separate from our mother and move out of the protection of the home toward the uncertainty of the father. Coming of Age is the first threshold we must cross to move out into the world of trials. Once we move from the security of the known we enter the unpredictable world of the masculine.

We are very powerful. We are the most dominant life form on the planet because of our highly evolved brain, not because of our physical power. In our culture we take longer than any other life form to leave the nest. There is a resistance, almost a fear of going out into the world of adventure because there is little clarity about whether we are prepared enough. The result of this resistance is we often go on the great adventure of life itself more frightened than excited.

In a conscious culture the young novice is prepared for life and this process is clearly acknowledged as a step toward individuality and freedom. Their tutoring is turned over to an elder, who, in most cases, the student has chosen. The teaching and discipline come from an objective and highly regarded member of the community who everyone respects. The tutoring allows the apprentice to continue acquiring life skills without interrupting their nurturing and supportive alliance with their birth mother and father. To be accepted as an apprentice is a victory, a prize rather than unsolicited discipline.

"The magical child was too innocent for a world of competition, domination and betrayal. Our teenager was willing to sacrifice their magic to survive. We forget that we had to deny our magic in order to succeed."

Shamanic cultures use many simple techniques to train their initiates. Younger students lack patience because they have no experience of "readiness." A simple example is to give students an unripe closed green pinecone and ask them to open it without breaking it. After consideration they complain saying, "It is impossible to open without damage before it is ready." I remind them it is impossible for them to lead training and encounter groups before they are ready without damaging the participants. They carry the green pinecone around and are asked to look at it regularly while they are in training. Once the pinecone has matured and opened, they are ready to apprentice in their first training. The real beauty of this method is the lesson comes from nature, as it should, rather than from the teacher.

We avoid exploring our teenage years because these times conjure memories of our inadequacy, which results in many of us being incomplete with these issues. It was during this passage we faced, for the first time, issues of romantic relationships, friendship, trust, sex, authority, peer acceptance, material survival and being good enough. We avoid our teenage years because of the deeply buried negative emotions that are re-awakened. During these years fear, humiliation, inadequacy and doubt were common to our experience and steadily lowered our self-esteem.

Our magical child didn't have the experience it needed to succeed in the market place. The magical child was too innocent for a world of competition, domination and betrayal. Our teenager was willing to sacrifice their magic to survive. We forget that we had to deny our magic in order to succeed. When working through this passage let your teenager know that you now understand and accept them. Openly appreciate this denied aspect of yourself.

Around age 13 we experience genetic transformation so powerful our body can change on a daily basis. Our emotions and mind are in constant transformation. We are confronted for the first time with the expectations of others. We are faced with challenges that are beyond anything we have ever imagined. The differences between male and female become more obvious. Absent of elders, our culture today gives little guidance creating fertile soil for trauma and soul loss during this period.

In conscious shamanic cultures at puberty girls are told they personify the Great Mother. With great excitement they are told it is time to become a woman. They are tutored in the art of the feminine and reminded they will be enlightened with the power of procreation that has manifested all life on earth. The young women are taught that menstruation is the first step of creation and that the Great Mother gave birth to the earth in this same way. They are taught, "The Great Mother had her period and her red lava flowed creating the land. From this purification all other life has been created." There is no confusion or shame, only the recognition that they have "come of age."

In shamanic cultures young people are prepared for the struggle that often accompanies life's significant rites of passage. Ritualized tattooing, body piercing, fasting and isolation are used to acquire the physical strength and endurance needed to survive the transformations of life. Teaching plants are also used to allow boys and girls to investigate the fears and doubts of their unconscious and to explore the wonder of their inner landscape. Teaching plants are cultivated and ritualized by elder women who give them to pubescent boys in order to "civilize their male energy." Teaching plants are natural plants, which bring about a more feminine and harmonious consciousness.

The elders make a clear distinction between chemical substances made in laboratories and natural plants that have taken millions of years to evolve through the guidance of nature. Teaching plants are thought of as gifts and are used to heal illness in the same way our contemporary healers prescribe medicines. The great difference is that in a shamanic culture uncontrolled male energy is considered an illness. In our modern culture the illness of uncontrolled male energy has been made a way of life. The value of teaching plant rituals is they diminish ego by expanding consciousness. In our culture the ritual of giving a young boy a teaching plant, with guidance and encouraging ritual use, would be a crime. The teaching elder would be condemned. Contrast this with the pervasive use of behavioral medications being prescribed for today's young adults, especially the males.

For decades we have spent billions of dollars to firmly entrench in our consciousness that the use of these plants is criminal rather than medicinal. When young people use teacher plants within the context of spiritual ritual, they respect them rather than fear and abuse them. It is during the ages of 13 to 26 we first begin to explore altering our consciousness. Contemporary elders, however, often brand youth who do this as criminals for doing what is natural. These elders have failed to fulfill their responsibility as teachers.

At this age our need to alter our consciousness may be evolutionary. During this time most of us explored or abused drugs and alcohol for the first time. Our ancestors used teaching plants to move through difficult passages like Coming of Age and Mid-Birth as ways to expedite their evolution. Teaching plants were highly regarded, which is why our ancestors cultivated them for thousands of years before we cultivated plants for food.

In our culture there is an emphasis on the criminal trafficking of these substances. Some politicians challenge the emphasis on the sinful supplier and propose we eliminate the demand. What everyone seems to miss is that the demand for teacher plants may be evolutionary and can only be understood through education by someone who has experienced that evolution. Someone that is respected rather than just another ignorant authority telling everyone to "just say no." Only an elder who has traveled the journey of many worlds is capable of teaching the dangers and healing powers of teaching plants.

Elders are less subjective than birth parents and come from a perspective of clarity rather than expectation. This objective distance, tempered with compassion, allows them the objectivity essential for successful mentoring. Primarily this passage is about new beginnings. The students are consciously being prepared to survive the trials and tests of life.

Passage 3 ~ Separation from the Feminine

A Time for Separation

"My mother and I hugged frequently. Italians do that, but as I grew older, I became stiff and would shun her embrace unless it was in the privacy of our home."

My Story About Separation from the Feminine

As a young boy I was shy and sensitive. Because I was quiet and soft for a while my father feared I was gay. To survive the violence at home and in the streets, I had to learn to talk and act tough. At puberty the most painful separation for me was the denial of young Francis, the timid child who had learned to compensate for poor vision by developing my other senses. I learned to read unspoken words beneath the meaningless chatter people use to cover their real thoughts. I was able to identify friends from long distances based on their body language. I knew when people lied from the lack of experience in their voice. I cultivated these and other abilities so Francis could survive. This process eventually included the denial and destruction of my magic.

Going to school without getting mugged was a challenge. Each day I changed my route to and from school to avoid being beaten by the older boys. To compound my problems, my mother and other family members called me Francis. To this day, those few who call me Francis evoke the sensitive me, but this name always initiated schoolyard abuse. I was teased constantly with "he-haw, he-haw" after the popular

Donald O'Connor movie series "Francis the Talking Mule." I handled this by insisting everyone, except my mother, call me "Frankie" in tribute to Frank Sinatra. I combed my hair back like Elvis and, like Marlon Brando in "The Wild Ones," I wore a black leather motorcycle jacket with a large skull and cross bones and Frankie painted across the back. From that day on my tough guy image hid gentle Francis and the schoolyard abuse stopped.

Other than Sunday picnics and the occasional summer day at the seashore, living in New York didn't involve spending much time in nature. Separating from nature was not an issue for me, but separating from my birth mother was difficult. My mother was the martyr and victim who was always there whether I was ill, hungry or just needed attention. My mother's sharp wit and dark humor was always good for a laugh. She was either a lot of fun or deeply buried in her victimhood. When she was depressed, I would ignorantly attempt to rescue her. As an adult, I learned she was diabetic and manic-depressive. If I had known this as a boy, I would not have taken her frequent mood swings so personally.

> *"Our excitement for life's adventure is not a personal attack against our mother or anyone else. We are simply becoming self-sufficient. This is not a problem. This is progress."*

My mother and I hugged frequently. Italians do that, but as I grew older, I became stiff and would shun her embrace unless it was in the privacy of our home. One day I was hanging out with the neighborhood guys showing off to the girls how macho we were. All of a sudden, my mother comes by and surprised me with a hug. Embarrassed by her public display of affection, I pushed her away. I knew that I had hurt her feelings, but realized in that moment the need to separate from her, something that was painful for both of us.

My Wisdom About Separation from the Feminine

We separate from our nature and our mother and leave the comfort and safety of the feminine. We cross the first threshold and enter the unpredictable world we were prepared and trained to enter. We have been trained physically, emotionally and mentally to separate. Eagerly, we leave the nurturing and safety of our home and move into the often harsh and cold reality we are now expected to master.

Coming of Age is a difficult passage because our mothers often take our enthusiasm for leaving them personally. Our excitement for life's adventure is not a personal attack against our mother or anyone else. We are simply becoming self-sufficient. This is not a problem. This is progress. The separation becomes personal when the mother does not recognize the need to quit her daily role of nurturer and thus forces the teenager to terminate her. This is when we need to be independent, no matter how lonely that becomes. Consciously and unconsciously, we reject our mother and deny everything that is vulnerable within ourselves.

In our male dominated culture young girls also decide they do not want to be like their mother. They begin to value and achieve what men do. In a shamanic culture this is normal predictable behavior. "In order to take root and blossom," it is said. "The pine cone must fall and roll away from the protective shade of the mother tree and into the light of the father, the sun."

Most of the changes in our thinking and behavior while separating from the feminine are minor, but collectively these changes have a major impact on our physical look, behavior and life plan. These physical and attitudinal shifts are only the tip of the iceberg. What lies beneath is our rejection of the earth, of nature and our feminine energy. Everything on earth has come from the great mother. Both males and females are born from and raised by women. Until coming of age, young boys are as sensitive and vulnerable as any girl. The young male, however, soon becomes desensitized as part of their conditioning to survival as a male.

In the time of mythology, the "hero's quest" was always a male adventure. There are two schools of thought about why this was. The first is women have already received the gift of wholeness. They don't need to go on any quest. The second is mythology existed in a man's time, a chauvinistic time, when women were not respected enough to be characterized as heroes. Forty thousand years ago, before his-story, during the goddess years both men and women honored the values we now call feminine. They valued peace, preservation and partnership. The women of the goddess years represented these values almost genetically and displayed them in the confidence of her character and the way she spoke, walked and conducted herself. Women already had everything men were seeking, so they seldom went on quests.

In our modern culture women tend to agree and identify with male values. By doing so they have agreed to value domination over cooperation and competition over partnership. They use and discard rather than preserve. They value independence over relationship. This alliance with the masculine causes modern women to go through similar passages as men.

The result is our culture has given birth to women who are willing to create a new model. In this new model women do have the need for a quest, which is: 1) to embrace fully their feminine nature, 2) to value themselves as women, and 3) to heal the deep wound of male domination. This new model is accomplished by:

A Return to the Great Mother – Through honoring and returning home to earth and our bodies we reject the male systems that tend to dominate our religions. Descend from the lofty celestial focus of male-dominated religion and to accept the wonder and magic of the wisdom within nature.

Honoring the Denied Feminine – Acknowledge and honor home, partnership, nurturing, service, passion, healing and sex. Both men and women have allowed what we value most to be taken for granted.

Healing the Wounded Masculine – Men have dominated women for six thousand years. Most women have grown to distrust men and to distrust and deny their own male energy. Most women have embraced male values just as men have. Most women have been betrayed by those values just as men have. This betrayal has not been by men, but by the values of male domination that women have accepted.

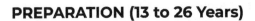

Passage 4 ~ Sexual Initiation

Follow Your Passion

*"For a kid buried in Catholic dogma having
shameless sex in the late 1950s was difficult.
In time I became more playful, which is the
best way I know to move past shame."*

My Story About Sexual Initiation

I've enjoyed my share of sex, but as an adolescent I had no guidance.
I played house and doctor with friends but don't recall ever discussing
sex with my parents.

My coming of age was from the mid 50s to the early 60s. I was
fortunate during this time that the whole world seemed to be coming of
age in what would eventually be called a sexual revolution. I went from
a young aspiring Italian Catholic boy to sex, drugs and rock n' roll.
The opportunity to explore love freely opened me to pleasures I would
enjoy the rest of my life.

Many of us have had embarrassing or even traumatic sexual experiences because we were not prepared. Looking back my first sexual experiences were humorous though, as a typical self-conscious teenager,
at the time they were humiliating. For a kid buried in Catholic dogma
having shameless sex in the late 1950s was difficult. In time I became
more playful, which is the best way I know to move past shame. Once
I was in bed with my girlfriend, but for whatever reason I couldn't perform. I joked that maybe there were more people in bed than just the

two of us. So, we began to visualize all of them. We named our parents, her ex, my ex, the church, government and anyone else we could think of who would not approve. We then proceeded to exorcise all we visualized from the room and went on to enjoy a wonderful experience.

One great relationship began as friends when I was 17 years old and lasted decades (as adults we'd discuss our spiritual insights as we had both grown older and more meta-physical). I remember going to her house and meeting her parents. In those days that was a customary ritual before leaving the house. It was a warm summer evening so we rushed to Manhattan Beach, removed our clothes and played under the stars. When we went back to where we had left our clothing everything was gone. We panicked, covered ourselves with a blanket and, laughing hysterically, took a taxi to some friends who loaned us money and clothing. When we returned to her house, we expected to be cross-examined about why we were late and wearing a change of clothing, but her parents remained warm and friendly, pretending that they did not notice anything. I remember wishing I had parents like that.

As a young art student, I entered the Fashion Institute of Technology where I was initiated into fashionable sex. It was a wild school filled with talented artists and models from all over the United States and Europe. There were about 1,800 students with 300 males and half of those were gay. I studied fine arts but spent time with the fashion crowd because they were the most fun. I shared a fancy brownstone in the West Village with my friends Antonio Lopez and Juan Ramos. My roommates threw lavish parties and the house would be filled with New York art influencers like Oleg Cassini and Leo Castelli along with beautiful models surprised to discover that I was straight.

"We live in a world of ideas and, when we adopt these ideas as true, we manifest a life consistent with the ideas we have embraced. When we are brought up with ideas of shame and guilt, shame and guilt are what we create."

My Wisdom About Sexual Initiation

There are many sexual initiations other than our first experience as we are introduced to a range of emotions that range from embarrassment to trance-like ecstasy. Many new sexual points of view confront the values of our youth. We live in a world of ideas and, when we adopt these ideas as true, we manifest a life consistent with the ideas we have embraced. When we are brought up with ideas of shame and guilt, shame and guilt are what we create. There are shamanic cultures whose language does not include those words. What would it be like to live in a society where shame and guilt do not exist? Imagine that.

One of the requirements for sexual satisfaction is our willingness to be present. This is easy when we are inspired by passion. When distracted, however, being present is impossible. There are shamanic cultures with no language for past and future. In their world all they know is the moment. When our thoughts are in the past or the future, we are not present. Instead, we are lost in our regrets or expectations.

Our willingness to be present is the most important ability for living a satisfying spiritual and sexual life. Spirituality and sexuality have a great deal in common. Present time is the domain of both spirit and passion and, to live spiritually, it helps to be passionate. After many sexual initiations I realized that sex at the height of orgasm is an energetic phenomenon that transcends the physical where we may enter the world of spirit. In this moment, when we are willing, we don't have a body or an identity. The ego disappears. We may not know where we are. Imagine sharing with your partner that you experienced ecstasy so powerful that you left your body. Imagine, upon return, celebrating the experience of spiritual unity achieved though intimacy and your willingness to be present.

"Many people withhold their feelings because we have been taught to fear our passion. This suppression creates victimhood. We live in a culture that tends to punish the passionate and reward the reasonable."

For a teenager in our culture sex is rarely presented as a spiritual experience. Instead, sex is usually seen as a hormonally driven love obsession, an act of control or conquest, an orgasm, or fear of unwanted babies and disease. As we move into adulthood, achieving positive sexual beliefs and learning to let go are essential to having a harmonious and satisfying sex life. Otherwise, we risk being stuck in outworn behavior and unconsciously burdened like the person in this story: "A traveler comes to a river. Looking for a way to the other side, she discovers a canoe and paddles across. On the other side all she can see ahead of her is a barren desert. Stuck in the last belief of a successful crossing, rather than leaving the canoe behind, she drags the canoe along as she begins her journey into the desert." It is essential that we acknowledge who and what has served us, to learn to let go and move on unburdened and empowered.

As teenagers we are confronted with how to live our sexuality. Most of what we feel is insecurity coupled with sexual curiosity. Many people withhold their feelings because we have been taught to fear our passion. This suppression creates victimhood. We live in a culture that tends to punish the passionate and reward the reasonable. The real issue is not the fear of our passion, but fear of poor sexual performance and the insecurities of incompetence.

Coming of age is when sexual rites of passage become a priority. Yet our culture has betrayed its responsibility to provide competent sexual education. We have been so programmed to fear our passion that few of us relate to our sexuality in a confident way. As evidenced in conscious shamanic societies, during "pre-history" goddess cultures both women and men were taught to understand, honor and respect their sexuality. These cultures offered a holistic approach that elevated sex to a responsibility and passage to spiritual experience. In our modern culture for far too long sexual preparation and education have been the blind leading the blind in schoolyards or the back seats of cars.

After years of exchanging passion, I designed a ritual called the Touch of Passion where the receiver goes into deep trance and experiences orgasmic energy throughout their entire body. This occurs without guilt, confusion, shame, penetration, pregnancy or disease. Through the ritual we experience the difference between passion and orgasmic energy. Rather than another pleasant sexual encounter, we experience sex within the context of a sacred ritual that honors the natural course of energy.

"The purpose of passionate sex is to experience pleasure and delight, an ecstatic way to exchange and share life force. Passion is the powerful primal force of the physical world, the energy that both creates and destroys form."

The flow of orgasmic energy is a spiritual experience. Neither a partner nor self-stimulation is required, only the surrender or absence of ego. In shamanic cultures exchanging passion and the conception of a child are two very different acts. One is adult recreation and the other is done with the knowledge and guidance of the elders. When we have sex for the purpose of childbirth, we cease having sex with just our partner and invite the participation of Spirit. We are giving physical form to Spirit. We are reincarnating. Conception is not something we do on our own.

The adult play of exchanging passion in a shamanic culture is quite different from sex for the purpose of procreation. The purpose of passionate sex is to experience pleasure and delight, an ecstatic way to exchange and share life force. Passion is the powerful primal force of the physical world, the energy that both creates and destroys form. Our need to express passion comes from an instinctive awareness that when we withhold it passion becomes anger. Cultural disapproval is not the only reason we withhold our passion. We unconsciously fear rather than consciously respect that power. We have witnessed many people and groups that have been destroyed by their inability to express their passion appropriately. We often show respect for our own passion by withholding it or distancing ourselves from it, which results in our being afraid of the very power we secretly respect and desire.

In our culture "follow your passion" is a common refrain, however, this is rarely encouraged. In most organizational structures those who resist following their passion are rewarded for being stable and reliable. Individuals who follow the call of their passion are seen as noncompliant. This is why so many secretly whisper about their passionate experiences as if they have done something wrong or sinful. If we believe that sex is dirty then we are also dirty because the act of sex created us. How can we ever be whole when deep inside we believe that we were created through a sinful act and were wrong on arrival?

The business of religion is to redeem the sinner. To redeem sinners, religion must create sinners. To create sinners our religious leaders fabricated unattainable ideals and passed them on to us as the word of God, rather than the mere ideas of earthly men. Rather than create our own sexual values and beliefs we remain sinners for only as long as we believe their dogma. The endless battle between religion and sex has to do with the power of passion and the realization that, rather than suffer the dogma of religion, we can have a spiritual experience through sex.

Sex is natural and possesses the power to heal. Sex should be sold in health food stores. Sex should be enjoyed in nature rather than some heart shaped bed with a mirror on the ceiling. In nature sex loses its significance and all the psychobabble we attach to it. Surrounded by the wonders of nature, we realize how small and insignificant we are. Our innocence and playfulness return when we realize how we are simply another animal playing on the surface of our Great Mother. This passage invites us to follow our passion and dance with the force of life, the destroyer and creator of all things and allow her to lead us into ecstasy.

INITIATION (26 to 39 years)

Passage 5 ~ Alliance with the Masculine

Pass the Test

The Second Triad: Initiation

During Alliance with the Masculine, we go out into the world of the workplace to compete and win. This passage may also be considered our "Father Quest" and occurs around the age of 26 (2 x 13 years) and begins the journey through the Second Triad: Initiation that includes Passage 6 ~ Realization of Betrayal and Passage 7 ~ Mid-Birth, which begins as early as age 39 (3 x 13 years).

> *"The house hummed with lectures and fresh ideas. Everyone was working on expanding their consciousness not because they were sick but because that is the only game worth playing. This simple concept transformed my life."*

My Story About Alliance with the Masculine

I was walking down Broadway in my signature black attire when I saw people standing in line at 78th Street. I asked what was happening and they said, "Psychodrama, it's like a psychotherapy play." Curious, I went inside the theater and sat on the back row. On the stage people began to play out their personal dramas. I was fascinated and kept going back. One evening the director, an older gentleman, pointed at me and said, "You! You haven't said a word. What do you want?"

I responded, "Man, leave me alone, I'm just watching." The director was Jacob Moreno, the creator of psychodrama. Soon I was up on the stage acting out my life in front of thirty people. I experienced an immediate and profound shift in my perspective and went on to become a psycho-dramatist playing antagonist, mirroring, and doubling participants. The work was enlightening and rewarding. Moreno encouraged me to come out of my shell. Psychodrama brought forth a part of me that was outgoing and vibrant, an experience that altered the course of my life and work. Moreno's epitaph reads: "The man who brought laughter to psychiatry."

By the age of 24 I had moved to California and become a Synanon Encounter Master responsible for encounter groups and the four hundred San Francisco Bay Area "Synanon Game" players who came to express their feelings each week at our Embarcadero warehouse. I worked with returning Viet Nam veterans at Oak Knoll Naval Base. The University of California at Berkley hired Synanon as consultants. That is where I met Bucky Fuller who regularly visited our Tomales Bay facility and brought the 60s Esalen crowd who exchanged their wisdom for ours. The house hummed with lectures and fresh ideas. Everyone was working on expanding their consciousness not because they were sick but because that is the only game worth playing. This simple concept transformed my life.

> "At the age of 28 I co-founded Phoenix House
> in New York, which went on to become the largest
> drug-free rehabilitation community in the world.
> When you are responsible for a community as large as
> eighteen-hundred people there are many therapeutic
> structures you can create to enable self-awareness."

At the age of 28 I co-founded Phoenix House in New York, which went on to become the largest drug-free rehabilitation community in the world. When you are responsible for a community as large as eighteen-hundred people there are many therapeutic structures you can create to enable self-awareness. Phoenix House was a twenty-four hour a day therapeutic community so there was always a lot to do. Everyone was engaged, purposely kept busy and overworked. That caused them to complain there was not enough time to do everything. As an experiment I changed all of the clock faces from a 24-hour day to a 30-hour day. At first there was the predictable chaos and then people reported that they had more time to get things done.

Phoenix House experienced incredible growth and, at one point, the staff became title crazy. I called a general meeting and announced that all titles would be discontinued. Instead, we would initiate new titles inspired by Medieval Europe: directors became kings and queens; assistant directors, dukes and duchesses; middle management lords and ladies and administrative staff became the serfs, etc. We had wizards, who arrived unannounced at any of the fifteen communal sites, assigned to stop everything and pull people out of their unconscious routines. The wizards could make the dishwasher the facility director king/queen for the day or the automotive crew the kitchen staff. My phone rang off the hook with questions like, "What does a duke do?" My response, "The same thing you did yesterday when you were assistant director."

During this exercise we learned a lot about ego, the difference between personal power and vested power and our inherent resistance to change. And it was a lot of fun. Life was never boring in the early years of Phoenix House, which is why the residents stayed until they were rehabilitated. Eventually the board of directors became disenchanted with my untraditional methods and behavior. Phoenix House began to devolve into a bureaucracy. We began to lose key people. At the time I was married, earned a good salary, had a pension, respect, authority, a driver and all of the other success symbols a young man could want. The board of directors, however, continued to frown on my use of meditation, bonding and other innovative therapies.

I went to so many Phoenix House board meetings that I became bored. I recall thinking if this was success, I needed to change the definition. What followed was an endless barrage of bureaucratic nonsense that robbed my clinical staff of their power. My energy and interest shifted toward more creative business activities like production of music and TV commercials. Ultimately, I resigned after thirteen years as co-founder and clinical program director. When innovation gives way to procedure I'm usually gone. I left because, among other reasons, Phoenix House had become the bureaucracy it was created to replace.

While at Phoenix House I received awards from the New York Board of Education, the New York Mayoral Award, a West Point Academy commendation and public service medals from the Hollywood Radio, TV & Film Society. I appeared frequently on television and radio programs and in newspaper articles. After thirteen years at Phoenix House the recognition I value most is that I was part of a team that created a dream that exists to this day and heals thousands of people each year.

Following my resignation, I took a year off to recharge my batteries and rediscover what success was for me. As a compulsively driven and passionate person I rented a studio on East 81st where I painted every day until at least one o'clock in the morning. My wife came to disapprove of my behavior and filed for divorce.

During this period, after working at the studio, I hung out at Elaine's on the Upper East Side. Elaine Kaufmann became a supportive friend through my marital problems and departure from Phoenix House. She was the first to purchase one of my new paintings and hung it in her restaurant. She sat me at the round VIP family table in the front of the restaurant where I enjoyed conversations with literary figures such as Mario Puzo, Noel Behn, Dan Jenkins, Shel Silverstein and Tennessee Williams.

A survivor of the New York streets herself, Elaine introduced me to New York celebrities and high society. This time, unlike my earlier experiences in the superficial fashion world, I didn't feel like the onion at the table. I was accepted and respected for my work with Phoenix House and my art.

One evening Elaine asked me to join some of her guests for a drink. The party included Jacqueline Kennedy Onassis. The former first lady eventually turned to me and said, "Elaine tells me you do incredible work with people in trouble with drugs, tell me about it." I began to talk and learned Jackie was very interested in meditation. Her companion kicked me under the table to shut me up, but Jackie kept asking questions and I kept answering. That evening I remember thinking how that conversation was quite a leap form the hostile racist dinner rhetoric back home in Brooklyn.

A year passed. I took a job as a trainer for Actualizations because other trainers had difficulties with what they called "New Yorker hostility." Since I was born and raised in New York, this was not a challenge for me. I left after nine months because, once again, there was limited space for creativity or innovation.

I agreed that I would never work for anyone again. In 1979 I founded The Natale Institute (TNI) in Houston, Texas. In those days Houston was a boomtown and a fun place to live. I designed my craft as a teacher and a group leader. It was in Houston that I created the Life Skills trainings, The One Experience and wrote Manifesting Results. From a handful of very supportive friends and an answering machine within two years TNI had its own training building attracting thousands of participants from across the United States. The governor of Texas honored me with a Texas Flag, but my favorite award was being made an Admiral in the Texas Navy. Houston became TNI headquarters and we grew to have area directors in Miami, Austin, Los Angeles, San Francisco, Tulsa, Boulder and Denver.

The value of those ten years in Houston was the people I met in Texas and around the country. A hundred names come to mind and all of them became great friends. The relaxed South and Midwest ways taught me how to hang out and be a friend. After ten years, once again, success required administrative skills and being a public person, which robbed me of my creative time and privacy.

Ultimately, I fulfilled the Father Quest and discovered what I value.

This book is about my wild ride and the lessons I have learned traveling the Circle of Life. When we overcome the fear of having nothing, of truly letting go of everything, a trust in life itself manifests the peace we seek.

"When we work with passion it leads us to excellence. When we don't, we risk the worse fate possible, which is to become successful at something we hate."

My Wisdom About Alliance with the Masculine

This is the time for slaying dragons, making our mark on the world and being good enough. We begin to acquire practical power for the first time. We buy homes and begin businesses. Couples marry and start families. The young adult is born. Suddenly we focus on a material world that we may have rejected in our early life. The most common complaint about fathers: "He was not there enough." My response to this has always been, "No, he wasn't. If he was there, he would have been your mother." When we separate from our nature, we lose the symbols of the earth, which are feminine and nurture us. When we move toward our father we move toward the sun, which is masculine and protects and warms us from a distance.

During this passage we feel a need to come closer to our father. There is a desire to experience that relationship, to resolve and heal it and in order to do that we must come closer to his way and his point of view. As we begin to duplicate him, we begin to understand and accept him. If we remain angry about his absence during our childhood, or the way he parented, we become stuck in judging him and competing with him rather than healing these biased memories. An attitude of getting even with our father hurts us more than him as we miss mastering important issues around authority, work values and the acquisition of skills.

Work is the way we contribute to the world, our family, and community. It is a demonstration of all the skills we have learned since our birth. It is how we show the world we are capable and how the world is willing to compensate us. When we work with passion it leads us to excellence. When we don't, we risk the worse fate possible, which is to become successful at something we hate. When we work with passion our work has purpose and direction. Otherwise, we work out of a fear-based need to be accepted and "good enough" for our parents, spouse, children or our community. Instead of being self-determined we respond to everyone else's needs. We are literally trying to be someone else (our father, mother, coach, guru, etc.). Eventually we realize it's easier to follow our own passion and simply be ourselves.

"We value thinking more than feeling and surrender our basic instincts until we no longer trust our feelings. Money, fame and power become our symbols of success."

During this passage we become obsessed with the world of the masculine and start to think competition rather than cooperation. We value thinking more than feeling and surrender our basic instincts until we no longer trust our feelings. Money, fame and power become our symbols of success. Blinded by what our new friends promise we may lose track of old friends. Some people attempt to raise their children better than their parents raised them, like they have something to prove, rather than realizing that being a better parent is the least we can do.

Ultimately everything has a price tag. We begin to question ourselves: "What is the point? Is all of this stuff really going to make me happy? Or is it just more stuff?" Around the age of 39 our first "Realization of Betrayal" happens. At the time we believe we can control the physical, emotional, and mental rollercoaster that follows. With time we recognize that we may have no control whatsoever, that this betrayal is just the first of a series of mid-life revelations.

Passage 6 ~ The Realization of Betrayal

The Illusion of Success

Betrayal happens when we love and trust others more than ourselves. It happens when we project our hopes and dreams onto others with the expectation that they may save us in some way. It occurs when we become so reckless that our relationships lose respect for us and can no longer handle the burden. Betrayal occurs when we are willing to be a victim. The Realization of Betrayal begins when we suspect that the rewards of success will not be delivered. We begin to question our values and ask, "For whom am I doing all of this?" This passage usually occurs around age 39 (3 x 13 years) or later.

My Story About Betrayal

In art school there was never any sympathy for being betrayed, only the pretense of adulthood that made betrayal a game. Barbara and I were young lovers. She worked a modeling job and one night, foolishly, I followed her home. As I had suspected, another lover arrived. I waited, sitting on the steps outside of her apartment listening to their laughter and passion. Lost in my drama I didn't hear that they were leaving. In humiliation I covered my face. They continued to talk as they went down the stairs. I have no idea if she knew that I was sitting there on those steps. We never discussed it. I acted as if it never happened. Maybe for her it never did. Soon after that we drifted apart. For many years this impacted my romantic relationships and willingness to trust.

My father told the story of how his older brother took advantage and stole the family business that, according to my father, was to be shared equally with all of the brothers. His story of betrayal influenced me. Later in life, fearful that I would be betrayed, I played out similar roles with business partners by encouraging apprentices to betray me, go out on their own and prematurely end our agreements.

There were many events in my professional life that I experienced as betrayal: being forced out of Phoenix House, a troubled business partner in Europe who sent the police to arrest me on false charges, or associates who plagiarized my intellectual and creative property. In retrospect, those perceived betrayals forced me to get out of my comfort zone into new initiations. They forced me to move on and create the new life experiences I secretly desired.

While in the void of betrayal I would lie around a lot thinking about death. I began projects that within hours held no energy or purpose. I was buried in the chaos of mid-life crisis. Business partners questioned my competence. Family questioned my sanity. They were right and, although I loved them, I did not listen because these were the same people and opinions I wanted to release.

> "There is not one major betrayal that causes us to question the meaning of life. It is most often the accumulation of years of disappointments, broken promises, losses, and unfulfilled expectations."

My Wisdom About Betrayal

Betrayal is easy to find. It runs rampant in affairs of the heart and is normal in most business situations. To transcend this, and not get caught up in revenge, remember the immediate shock and sadness you experienced when you felt betrayed. Instead, consider the empowerment found in honesty and integrity. There is not one major betrayal that causes us to question the meaning of life. It is most often the accumulation of years of disappointments, broken promises, losses, and unfulfilled expectations. The value in this process is realizing the opportunity to redefine what it means to succeed. We begin to question everyone and everything in our life. What was once important to us may become meaningless. We find ourselves surrounded by material possessions we no longer value. We remain in exhausted relationships because we are dependent on them emotionally or financially.

We find ourselves in a void of nothingness where everything in and around us seems to be failing. Everything we have achieved becomes irrelevant or trivial. Worst of all there are no new pictures. We are stuck, unable to foresee anything in our future. We have questioned what we value many times, but that is not what frightens us. What terrifies us is looking toward our future and seeing nothing except a profound sense of non-existence that our un-evolved self perceives as death. It takes time to manifest new values. Understand that such a transformation, such a complete letting go, requires time to give form to our new values and our new life.

"We call this passage the mid-life crisis because we have agreed that material wealth and youthful beauty are the ultimate symbols of success."

My advice to anyone going through this passage is to give yourself a break. Don't do anything. Evaluate what is happening and learn how to let it be. As much as you would like to run away, don't do it. Don't quit your job or leave your relationship. Just hang in there because you will have plenty of time if that's appropriate. While in this passage it seems that there are no solutions and that no one can help you. The best you can do is to survive what you are going through. It is essential to hold your ground and observe the tempest of chaos swirling around you. Arrive at a place where you can smile and say, "My lover just left, I totaled my car, my teenage daughter is pregnant, and my business is bankrupt – but I'm okay."

We love our family and friends, but also wonder what life would be like without them. We value our career and the security of our job at the same time we long to do something else. As we transform, we become frightened because everything we once relied upon is up for grabs. Everything is in question. We call this passage the mid-life crisis because we have agreed that material wealth and youthful beauty are the ultimate symbols of success. As our direction shifts from the physical to the meta-physical, we realize that all along we have been struggling to be good enough. We have been unconsciously working to pay some kind of karmic debt.

Conscious shamanic cultures expect this passage. The family and community support Mid-Birth individuals with unconditional love. The Elders understand this passage and that the person will be bouncing off walls and exhibiting crazy behavior for at least a year. When we accept this, we care for the loved one until they can take care of themselves like you would care for any newborn.

"This is a birth into our power and the beginning of a series of life changes that cause us to become more and more like ourselves. Suddenly, it seems foolish to waste our time and energy to satisfy the expectations of others."

There were shamanic cultures that did not allow men to marry until after they were forty years of age because, until after mid-life, male energy was considered too uncivilized. Other shamanic cultures would not allow men under forty to know the secrets of their religion because they believed men would not realize the true meaning until they had completed this passage. Unlike our physical birth, which is unconscious, Mid-Birth is a spiritual birth and totally conscious. We see and feel everything. Nothing is overlooked. This is a birth into our power and the beginning of a series of life changes that cause us to become more and more like ourselves. Suddenly, it seems foolish to waste our time and energy to satisfy the expectations of others. Becoming more and more true to ourselves is all we are willing to do.

Mid-Birth is the first time most of us really experience our mortality. We consider the inevitability of our death and reluctantly prepare to journey toward the meta-physical. Material power and possessions die with the body. What we need to acquire at mid-life is spiritual power, but first we must unload the extra baggage. Letting go is difficult because, in our modern Western culture, who are we without these people and possessions? If we resist a spiritual persecution occurs and we are forced to let go, forced to transform as our lover leaves, we lose our job, or our health fails. Spirit has a bizarre sense of humor. Often what we call an unfortunate circumstance becomes divine intervention.

> *"If we struggle to succeed and then become angry it is because we suffer from the illusion that life is unfair. Life is not fair. Life is abundant, but until the Mid-Birth passage we don't know that."*

After this struggle Mid-Birth becomes an opportunity for renewal. The corporate VP quits a high-paying position to teach at a local high school or college. The full-time homemaker starts their own business or goes back to school. Although these transformations may appear simple, beneath them the person has overcome significant challenges to arrive at a new way of life. If we struggle to succeed and then become angry it is because we suffer from the illusion that life is unfair. Life is not fair. Life is abundant, but until the Mid-Birth passage we don't know that. Instead, we suffer low self-esteem and begin to question and reevaluate our identity.

An alliance with the masculine leads us astray with the pervasive perks. Eventually we accept that we have somehow betrayed our truth. We realize that time is running out and become acutely aware of our dissatisfaction. We question goals that have not been achieved and doubt our unique identity. Everything is open to question and very few questions are answered. We feel betrayed.

After 30 years a dedicated worker finds their skills are no longer valued. Patriots become disillusioned that corruption is rampant throughout government and industry. National security becomes the excuse to scapegoat or kill. Fear becomes the currency of manipulation. We have compromised our environment to the point where we are an endangered species. Governments, corporations, and citizens commit ethical atrocities in the name of commerce or the greater collective good. We build toxic prisons euphemistically called cities. We endlessly march from one war to another, our values so confused we sacrifice our children, and their futures, for what someone else believes.

*"In our manic media-driven culture we
now experience this level of male crisis energy
as the stress of normal everyday life. This is
not normal or healthy or evolved."*

Possibly the worst betrayal is the promise of the rewards of old age. We are led to believe that if we succeed in school, choose the right profession, and marry the right person that, when we are older, we will enjoy a happy and peaceful life. But what seems to be true is that if we plan our life according to the common success formula, we will be disappointed, disillusioned, and eventually betrayed. These and countless other lies are the reasons for our betrayal. We have embraced male energy as a way of life. In shamanic cultures kinetic male energy was seen as a disease that needed to be calmed and channeled and only used in times of crisis. In our manic media-driven culture we now experience this level of male crisis energy as the stress of normal everyday life. This is not normal or healthy or evolved.

We have been conditioned by fear. Once we rationalize and embrace fear it becomes impossible to recognize our truth under any circumstances. Fear separates us from everything and promotes us becoming victims who are incapable of seeing the truth. "The Realization of Betrayal" transforms in the direction of our power when we realize that truth is not external. We are the truth. Fear has ruled this planet and our way of life for thousands of years. Fear continues uninterrupted and unchallenged. Once we accept the enormous weight of this lie, we are able to let go of fear and embrace ourselves as the truth. This transformation moves us beyond betrayal to Mid-Birth and into the realization of our power.

Passage 7 ~ Mid-Birth

Birth into Our Power

My Story About Mid-Birth

I was taken out of the Beverly Hills Hotel in a semi-comatose condition and moved to a friend's house where I spent a year lolling around and complaining. I had hit a spiritual brick wall. Then one morning, without warning, I jumped out of bed and danced around blasting the Rolling Stones song "You Can't Always Get What You Want." After a year immersed in my own misery suddenly everyone in my life was upset that I was happy.

> *"The five passages that follow Mid-Birth become less defined and blend in more feminine, fluid and natural ways. Our attention is on one passage, but that one passage causes us to consider the others that remain."*

My Wisdom About Mid-Birth

Mid-Birth is short and unexpected. It comes without warning. One moment we are in the depths of chaos and confusion, the next we become renewed and excited about life. We experience the death of our obsession with the physical world and return home to the spiritual. Our perceptions shift and we become more accepting, relaxed, and wise. The five passages that follow Mid-Birth become less defined and blend in more feminine, fluid and natural ways. Our attention is on one passage, but that one passage causes us to consider the others that remain. They overlap so that all five may occur simultaneously. We can reconnect with our denied feminine while discovering our truth as we atone with loved ones while sharing our wisdom and preparing for death.

What occurs right before Mid-Birth is the profound loss of almost everything. Our belief systems crumble as we find ourselves surrounded by people and possessions we no longer value. We literally feel we are dying because what we have identified ourselves as being no longer holds significance. Mid-Birth happens once we realize we have based our life on illusions and pop-culture propaganda. We are disappointed because we believed in the promises of others rather than our own truth. When we live in propaganda and lies, we live in fear. We worry about our relationship or that our employer will no longer value us. When we live in fear, we never experience our power or evolve toward our true potential because fear destroys our power. The passage from betrayal to Mid-Birth is often humiliating because in our forties we are decisive adults who have achieved success and then, suddenly, we are uncertain about most everything.

> *"Middle age is not the beginning of decline, but the time to accept and cultivate the highest in our selves. This is a pause to reexamine what we have done and what we will do in the future."*

Middle-aged people are often the most conspicuous and most powerful in our society. They are leaders in business, government, education, entertainment and the arts. They control the economy and make major decisions for the rest of the population. Yet they receive a great deal of tabloid media attention for their relationship problems, career frustrations and failures, their fear of aging and death. These problems are not really problems they are misperceptions, predictable events to be expected in adult life.

Middle age is not the beginning of decline, but the time to accept and cultivate the highest in our selves. This is a pause to reexamine what we have done and what we will do in the future. It's the time to give birth to our power as we actualize new dreams and accept that there are other dreams that may not come true. Careers change, divorce and remarriage are common. Women and men must deal with getting older, the death of parents and loved ones, and significant physiological changes. We reconsider all of our relationships as our interests shift and commitments change.

Youth worshipping popular culture promotes the idea we are over the hill at age 40 and almost dead at 60. This frightening picture means middle age is only a step away from old age. This picture is warped like a Coney Island funhouse mirror. We are constantly reminded it is better to be slim, athletic, and maintain a youthful appearance. We obsess about "what's new" on the material plain: home, car, clothing, partners, etc.

In modern culture, beauty and sex appeal are more important in a woman's life. This dubious double standard makes aging more difficult for woman. During the Goddess ages women were valued for their wisdom, power and beauty. With male domination our values shifted to only their beauty. This is documented in many ways and can be seen most clearly in our art. Women were once portrayed with long graceful hair, dressed in flowing gowns holding a sword and battle shield, sitting among lions and other wild animals. Then the symbols shifted to a fragile naked woman rising out of the sea as Venus the goddess of love. The devaluation of women is especially true for those who lack authenticity. Authentic identity is a sense of who we are and our place in society. Aging intensifies our need to sort out our true identity and make it visible.

In shamanic cultures the Mid-Birth passage is viewed as a profound birth into our power and, like our physical birth, we are protected. We are withdrawing from friends and family, rejecting material wealth, but the community is prepared and knows that this death of the material is followed by a resurrection into the powerful spiritual self. We are tolerated, protected and nurtured through this passage.

Many of the illusions we endure are grounded in dogmatic religious beliefs, but even more so in psychobabble, the jargon of Western mental and emotional healers who have a vested interest in our dependence upon them to guide us through the mid-life crisis. The psychobabble of professional healers calls this time of loss a depression, which is like calling a shovel an implement for soil penetration (rather than a shovel). Many people are terrified of change and transformation, the death of the familiar and dysfunctional. They are terrified of the new and unknown because they rely on healers who are unaware of the inevitable passages of the Circle of Life.

At Mid-Birth we do not anticipate the death and resurrection of our values and literally believe the end is near. I have worked with hundreds of people who thought they were going to die while in this passage. They believed they were having a heart attack or that they would not wake up in the morning. Absent of guidance they believed they would not survive and all they had accomplished in life was not worth preservation. What is clear is that all of these illusions are external. They are a choice. They are only experiences or thoughts to which we attach significance.

"Once we start asking these questions we have begun to move toward our power – not our cultural power, not our religious power, not even our family power – but personal power absent of attachment to anyone or anything."

When we recognize the inherent value, crisis is an opportunity for greater understanding. Crisis is spirit intervening to say, "Here's the experience of bankruptcy and survival, so you can learn to stop worshipping money." Whatever the crisis, spirit calls to teach us a lesson we have been avoiding. The signs have been clear, but avoided. The self-deception we experience prior to Mid-Birth is extreme and sometimes includes the loss of everything we have.

Suddenly everything is going wrong. Our health is down, our energy is low, our cash flow ebbs and, although we love our partner, their presence is secondary. What follows is a period of self-confrontation: "What am I doing? What is the purpose of my life? What do I value?" Once we start asking these questions we have begun to move toward our power – not our cultural power, not our religious power, not even our family power – but personal power absent of attachment to anyone or anything. It's a difficult passage because we have been misled to believe: "If I am not all of these people and possessions, I am nothing."

Mid-Birth is a full-blown life experience. Nothing about this passage is subtle. Our energy rises with zealousness not felt since youth. We celebrate our rebirth and, as our new direction becomes clear, excitement and enthusiasm fill our consciousness. At Mid-Birth we resurrect, confusion and inertia pass and the active work begins. The transformation is difficult because, although we have clarity about our new direction, some of the people that surround us do not. Few understand and some are angry for all the drama they experienced while we were lost and inactive.

A close friend at Mid-Birth wanted to get rid of all their possessions and travel the world. His wife wanted no part of his adventure. She wanted the house, the ranch, the horses, and a divorce. He gave it all to her, and left in a luxuriously converted Greyhound bus. A Parisian friend started dating younger men, going out to clubs and dancing all night. She had married very young, was abandoned by her husband and supported her children alone. Sowing her wild oats for the first time, she was more alive than I had ever seen her. Her teenage children were enraged and upset. At forty their mother was acting like she was their age. Her teenagers acted like dogmatic parents refusing to condone her behavior for the few months she needed to live out her unexpressed teenager. It should be clear that there is the possibility that we will not get a lot of support for our new direction, especially from those closest to us.

*"We have a choice, to either move on creating a
new life based on new values or fight the process
of maturity, finding ourselves immersed
in bitterness and resignation."*

Our youth worshipping culture overlooks spiritual growth later in life. We ignore the rewards of peace and completion and instead we go for superficial beauty and sexual prowess. Because of this orientation people passing through the chaos of mid-life look back struggling to reexperience old thrills instead of anchoring new perspectives and behavior that are consistent with their future. Middle age is a psychological and emotional upheaval until we discover our power. We have a choice, to either move on creating a new life based on new values or fight the process of maturity, finding ourselves immersed in bitterness and resignation.

Our task is to let go of the old perceptions and begin to look at the world through new eyes. In mid-life the parts of us that have been the least cultivated will call out the loudest. If we spent our lives at home with the family, we tend to go out and interact with the world. If we have been driven by the challenges of our career, we will be drawn by the need to be with our family and a less competitive lifestyle. In general, the last half of our life causes us to give less attention to success and more to our spiritual values. This shift is not easy and requires us to reorder our entire life.

Almost everyone I know has experienced Mid-Birth multiple times. We live in an age when major events occur so often that we are always transforming. The digital communications revolution is leading the way to a consciousness revolution. We are both the cause of this revolution and simultaneously at its effect. We are both the garden and the gardener. We watch our cultural values explode giving way to new standards and habits that crumble just as fast. Our world is in spontaneous combustion as we are created and recreated by each other. This rapid chain reaction has all the stress, confusion, and loss of Mid-Birth with the added twist of frequency.

Every day we are expected to be successful in a world we no longer understand. Suddenly we must change careers, seek new education and training, survive periods of unemployment and accept new points of view. We are faced with new questions like: What does it mean to be a family? What will it be five years from now? These are impossible to answer given the speed of our evolution. In every area of our life, amidst countless distractions, we are being asked to reshape our perspectives, accept new definitions, adopt more inclusive attitudes and learn how to cultivate an authentic identity. Most of us measured our personal worth by our steady, productive employment and the stability of our relationships. Now we are expected to find wisdom in a world that is very different from the one we once relied upon, a world of uncertainty.

"Ritual opens us to the opportunities that are always present during these waves of change. Ritual allows us to participate in the experience of transformation rather than be a prisoner of it."

Mid-life crisis was a relevant concept when we lived only one life in a lifetime. Today it is common to live out three and four careers and be with as many lifetime partners. Today the speed at which our technology and values transform requires many new beginnings preceded by as many deaths that we call crisis. Ritual grounding is helpful during these rapid transitions. Ritual opens us to the opportunities that are always present during these waves of change. Ritual allows us to participate in the experience of transformation rather than be a prisoner of it. Ritual is a time out, a pause that allows us to reconnect with our priorities and fully realize the possibilities of our new reality. As we explore this new millennium we must let go of the old codes and make way for the new potentials for humanity.

INTEGRATION (39 to 52 years)

Passage 8 ~ Reconnection with the Feminine

Finding the Lost Pieces of Self

Beginning of the Third Triad: Integration

When the celebration of Mid-Birth is complete, we begin the Third Triad: Integration that includes Passage 8 ~ Reconnection with the Feminine, Passage 9 ~ Initiation into the Truth and Passage 10 ~ Atonement. Collectively these passages prepare us for Spiritual Elderhood.

My Story About Reconnection with the Feminine

With my Mid-Birth rejuvenation, I moved to Amsterdam where I lived, worked, and traveled presenting seminars throughout Europe. We held retreats at the Goddess Temple I helped build atop a mountain overlooking the Mediterranean on the Spanish island of Ibiza. During this time, I was incredibly energized and creatively productive. My work flourished. I designed trainings, produced eight trance dance albums, performed as Professor Trance & The Energizers, wrote the book *Trance Dance: The Dance of Life* and made countless friends all over Europe who hosted training courses and celebrated our work.

In Europe, reverence for the environment and Native American wisdom was everywhere. I was inspired by this and ecology became my passion. My previous Life Skills trainings combined information with experience, which are essential ingredients for successful transformation. Our new enhanced mission evolved into providing participants with experiences of the natural world and that brought me to shamanism. I taught people to trance dance and soul hunt, trained hundreds of instructors to lead our courses, presented The Circle of Life and Touch of Passion workshops, and led teaching plant rituals. I made many journeys to the Mayan ruins and rain forests of Mexico and Guatemala. I experienced ayahuasca rituals in the Amazon and subsequently brought ayahuasca Jaguar Shamans to Europe.

"For years I had worked in New York, California, Texas and Oklahoma where, beyond the frantic sprawl of urban chaos, Native American culture and wisdom had existed for over a thousand years."

I came to shamanism as a researcher, a curious New Yorker from Brooklyn, seeking fresh ideas to deepen the experience in our trainings and seminars. For years I had worked in New York, California, Texas and Oklahoma where, beyond the frantic sprawl of urban chaos, Native American culture and wisdom had existed for over a thousand years. Now, living in Europe and discovering shamanism, I was totally in awe of what I was learning about conscious cultures and their transformative ritual practices. I came to trust and embrace the inherent natural magic.

Once again, I found myself living on the edge of life, but this time I had gone too far and lost sight of all normalcy. Life was more than I had ever dreamed: my work being taught all over Europe, my book *Trance Dance: The Dance of Life* was well received and Island Records signed my band Professor Trance & the Energizers. I spent most of my time at our mountaintop Goddess Temple on Ibiza, immersed in natural wonder, being creative and exploring new realities. Then, on a business trip to Germany, the police arrested me at my apartment in Berlin.

The German government had me under surveillance including undercover agents in the ayahuasca rituals I led with the Amazon Jaguar

Shaman. German officials declared me a cult leader and posted warnings on the Internet. They conspired with the national news media that aired interviews they edited and overdubbed to mislead the public. Der Spiegel magazine, the German equivalent of *Time*, published condemning articles. The German, French and Spanish governments and media discredited me. Many associates with whom I worked across Europe turned their backs.

By 1998 the German crusade against Scientology was used to persecute everyone in Europe involved with natural healing or a New Age alternative lifestyle. I was deemed to be "a cult leader with fifty or less followers," which I considered an insult since I had more close friends than that. Despite the obvious absurdity of this German inquisition, my partners and friends distanced themselves. My business, which had been flourishing, went into receivership. My relationship of four years dumped me via fax the same day I planned to move to Paris to live with her and her children. This time I totally broke down, my thoughts were constantly confused. I literally bounced off walls and, for the first time in my life, I felt totally alone. I hung photographs of supportive friends to remind me that I wasn't.

> *"I have always been able to survive and find value in those difficult passages, for they move us beyond our reasonableness and control. My life has been more than anything I ever imagined because I've been willing to step off the edge of my reality."*

I felt useless, so dis-eased that my health totally broke down. I thought I would soon die. Friends and doctors agreed, so I returned to the United States for the medical care I desperately needed. Dear friends like Michael Brockman and Ayman Sawaf opened their homes, hearts and bank accounts. I was afraid to die, but to my surprise, as I reviewed my life's accomplishments and relationships, I was satisfied and complete. It was also very clear that this sense of peace was the reward for having lived my life fully.

Amidst this dark period, I had forgotten that the process by which I create my dreams has always been to leave the comfort zone and experience those rites of passage that initiate me into the magical realm of transformation. I have always been able to survive and find value in those difficult passages, for they move us beyond our reasonableness and control. My life has been more than anything I ever imagined because I've been willing to step off the edge of my reality. The extraordinary lessons of life reveal themselves to those who are willing to receive them. This passage redefined my concept of success. It softened me and changed my values.

Although my health was still poor, at 60 years of age I married Ichiko who has stood by me and nurtured me through poverty and near death. My son Jason and I live together dissolving the distance our society has grown to accept as normal between father and son. I live in Hawaii, the paradise I always desired but was too busy making money to afford. My nomadic lifestyle has ended. Instead, I spend my time writing and producing music, which I always promised myself I would do. My body is a priority and I spend a great deal of time caring for it. The doctors are surprised that even my poor health slowly improves. Most of all, I cherish and am grateful for each moment I have to enjoy the gift of life.

For years I had traveled to exotic beaches and resorts, but it was during this passage that I realized that these vacations were really about returning to nature. At first this return was unconscious, but I realized I was returning to my inner nature. I began to simplify my vacations and traveled to the tropical rain forests of Central and South America. The sea, wind and mountains satisfied something primal within me. Eventually what I enjoyed most was working with nature, building a home with friends and family on the Spanish island of Ibiza. One to three months a year being in the silence of nature without a phone or electricity became my preference. Working outdoors transformed my body and cleansed my emotions and mind. I was able to just relax in my hammock in awe of the beauty of nature that surrounded me.

With this passage my metabolism mellowed and I became more at ease about sex. I had enjoyed an active and passionate life and, at age 53, the criteria for satisfaction transformed. Desire arose less frequently. Unlike a lot of men this was not a letdown, but accompanied by a great sigh of relief as this was the time to focus on other things.

"As we reconnect with our feminine, we call home those lost pieces of ourselves that were lost to trauma and denied while traveling the road of initiations. We accept who we are and the ways of others."

My Wisdom About Reconnecting with the Feminine

After Mid-Birth the passages that follow become less defined and tend to blend. We are often in all five of the last passages simultaneously. At Mid-Birth our mortality confronts us in real ways for the first time. From then on, we are confronted from time to time until our actual death. We let go of the illusions and lies of our youth and replace them with the acceptance of ourselves.

We forgive others more easily and accept our ignorance, which gives way to humor and understanding about the human condition. We are also more willing to share what we have rather than withhold to maintain a competitive edge. Passages eight through thirteen evolve as blended experiences rather than the definitive sequential passages of the first seven.

As we reconnect with our feminine, we call home those lost pieces of ourselves that were lost to trauma and denied while traveling the road of initiations. We accept who we are and the ways of others. Our life becomes more peaceful as we genuinely enjoy being ourselves. Our power is that we now know who and what we enjoy and what we are unwilling to be around. Our task is to sort this out without making others and ourselves wrong.

New interests develop and old ones are revived. Material wealth becomes less important and our attention is directed toward friends and values that have served us during the course of our life. We heal the alienation we acquired in our quest to be successful. Our judgments become unimportant compared to the acceptance and gratefulness we feel for our relationships, especially those long-term relationships that were there for us when we needed them. Remembering a dear friend's birthday or making time to play with a child becomes more important than another business deal.

A potent aspect of this passage is coming face to face with our integrity. At this point we are unwilling to compromise our integrity to look good. Although we accept others, we are not willing to be in partnership with people whose values conflict with ours. For me, Reconnection with the Feminine required about 13 years. The Natale Institute was an international network of partners and, as the business transformed, each deserved thoughtful consideration. I didn't know I was realizing my integrity until half way through the process.

"During this passage we begin to return to our truth and call home those parts of ourselves we denied in order to survive the traumas of growing up. Our feelings soften. We begin to mellow and open like a flower to the sun."

The conventional "change of life" myth promises despair, depression and an end to sexual enjoyment. For many women the opposite is true as guilt and fear of unwanted pregnancy are cast aside for a more satisfying sexuality. Most women report that their sex life has either improved or has become less important. We recognize it's never too late to change our lifestyle. Achieving new goals becomes important and requires focusing our energy.

During this passage we begin to return to our truth and call home those parts of ourselves we denied in order to survive the traumas of growing up. Our feelings soften. We begin to mellow and open like a flower to the sun. We are sincerely interested in others. Stress, anger and heavy emotional issues are exchanged for an increased joy for life and living.

For me the most difficult parts of this passage were confrontations with lovers, friends and business partners. In time, ultimately the relationships I truly valued were healed and strengthened. Most inspiring were those relationships that, after years of absence, were renewed because one of us would come to the aid of the other. Concern for another's welfare takes precedence over differences. This is the true meaning of friendship, something we understood as teenagers but forgot as we became obsessed pursuing the false promises of pride and success.

This passage is a return to the acceptance of our personal power. During our quest for success, we lost pieces of our soul surrendered to acquire vested power. There are two kinds of power: personal power and vested power:

Personal power is grounded in our experience, the wisdom and value we have extracted from significant life passages. It is our unique power and no one can take it from us. This is what we rely upon in times of crisis. Personal power comes from within and living life is the teacher. It's meta-physical and the source is our growing awareness.

Vested power is grounded in external reality such as titles, position, possessions, status, wealth and reputation. It makes no difference whether these were acquired through hard work, luck or laziness. Vested power is given to us and is easily lost or stripped away. It is physical and its existence depends on the agreement of our environment.

Passage 9 ~ Initiation into the Truth

Letting go of Illusions and Lies

"Being honest has become so repressed that it's most often perceived as aggression. Truthfulness has been replaced by being polite."

My Story About the Truth

My understanding of truth has expanded from the self-righteousness of believing I was right to the humility of knowing there is no truth, only points of view. I have often been accused of being too honest, too straight, too frank. Throughout my life I have been in trouble with authorities because I said too much.

At about the age of 10 I remember coming home late from playing with my cousin Peter. My mother was waiting, claimed I looked suspicious and demanded an explanation. "Peter and I were half naked, playing doctor," I said. "It was a major operation." My mother grabbed her chest as if in mortal pain. "Oh God," she cried. "Oh God." In that moment it became clear that truth can kill someone. I was not mature enough to know my mother was a drama queen. Instead, I thought that my truth had caused her suffering. After that experience when my mother asked, "What did you do today?" My reply would be "Nothing ma, nothing." She would check my fingers and eyes to see if they were there and say, "Go wash up, we're about to eat." That's really all she wanted to hear.

Rather than being rewarded, like most children, I received little encouragement for telling the truth. Kids don't learn to lie from other kids in the schoolyard. We learn to lie to avoid hurting loved ones and being hurt ourselves. As adults, long after we are capable of handling confrontation, we continue to habitually withhold our criticism from those close to us.

Being honest has become so repressed that it's most often perceived as aggression. Truthfulness has been replaced by being polite. With my mother I was never able to share the excitement I experienced growing up like jumping roofs, making out with girls, or being accepted by the local gang leader. Nor did I share that I thought she often tried to manipulate me with her victimhood. My mother and I missed the joy and laughter of honest communication. After her death I chose never to deprive myself of that level of experience. I am usually frank and straight, even when it hurts.

"When I first realized that there was no truth, I relaxed because I accepted that 'our truth' is nothing more than our mutual bullshit. Absolute truth does not exist on the physical plane. Here there is only the latest lie or my point of view vs. your point of view."

My mother once threatened to wash my mouth out with soap, a familiar refrain in the 50s. "If you do," I said. "I'll blow bubbles out my ass." I was often punished for being a wise guy, which I was. With parents, teachers, police, lovers, students and friends I have frequently managed to say too much. Whether sarcasm, or astute observation, it was seldom well received except for the few close friends who enjoyed encountering each other's limitations. I literally get high when I speak my truth, my consciousness releases and I feel lightheaded. When I first realized that there was no truth, I relaxed because I accepted that "our truth" is nothing more than our mutual bullshit. Absolute truth does not exist on the physical plane. Here there is only the latest lie or my point of view vs. your point of view.

One of the rewards of telling our truth is that when we do, we immediately find ourselves in present time. Whenever I visited my family after a long absence it was like traveling back in time. My sister talked as if it was years ago, about relatives I didn't even remember. I am always fascinated that people talk to you as if you are in the same place that you were when they saw you last. In the 90s, when I would return to New York I was still the Frank Natale who co-founded Phoenix House and helped heal thousands of people with chemical dependencies, who worked with the needy and the poor. When I explained I no longer do the drug rehabilitation work, that I teach seminars on life skills and shamanic healing, it's like I had said nothing and they refer drug addicts to me. With time I've learned to be less confrontational and tell the truth in playful ways.

"Life is filled with injustices and contradictions. This provides us with ample opportunity to play victim, blame and complain. There are no victims other than those who are ignorant or unaware of their choices."

My Wisdom About the Truth

After our share of deception in business, friendship and romance we are willing to let go of the great illusions and lies of our youth. Those include: romantic love, life is not fair, I'm not good enough, parents are people, life is a struggle, and I am independent.

Romantic Love – Romantic love guarantees suffering because it is based on ideals rather than partnership. It is something men do and most women want. Generally, men prefer tender loving care, which is more maternal than romantic. Men and woman are willing to sacrifice almost everything, even their spirituality, for that perfect romantic love with the expectation this will grant them everlasting joy.

Men invented romantic love and women believed it. Romantic love was a spiritual path created in 12th century France by the Troubadours to revive Goddess worship. Young men dressed in armor and charged on horses beneath the balconies of fair ladies shouting, "Amour, amour!" The difference between the romantic love of the Troubadours and our version of modern romantic love is that those worshipping Troubadours never consummated their desire. The French saw feminine energy as the path to spirit. The great cathedrals of the era were called Notre Dame du Paris, Notre Dame du Chartre. "Notre dame" means through the feminine.

Valuing romantic love over spiritual love is a new idea and not a good one. Having fallen in love a few times with French women I learned this lesson the hard way. In my lover's apartment in Paris, I remember passionately singing the classic song "When A Man Loves A Woman" over and over. At the time the lyrics became my mantra. Looking back, it's clear why in the end I felt victimized. I literally prayed to become the fool in misery.

"We believe that if we find the right lover our search will end. Given the choice between finding the perfect romance or the perfect spiritual path most people will choose the romance."

There is only one reason for falling in love and that's because it feels good. If I could reclaim all the hours, money, effort and intelligence that I've spent on meaningless romance today I would be more healthy, wealthy and wise. Romantic love is temporary, an illusion of well-being. It's narrow and obsessive and just another tunnel with no reward. When the romance falls apart, we go looking for another fix and another fix until we are living like a mouse sniffing out cheese in some cruel lab experiment. We become so foolish that each time another romance comes along we say things like "I've never met anyone like this before" or "this one is different."

When we buy into the lie of romantic love this cycle never ends. The lie is that we believe this person will make us whole. We believe that if we find the right lover our search will end. Given the choice between finding the perfect romance or the perfect spiritual path most people will choose the romance. While in love we surrender our heart and put our passion in prison. Then the manipulation and withholding begin, which always ends in pain.

In our culture, romantic love is based on the myth of Tristan and Isolde, one of the most depressing love stories ever written. It's about two lovers who are separated. Tristan is a knight assigned by his king and friend to protect Isolde, the king's wife. Instead, Tristan falls in love with Isolde. Guilt-ridden Tristan and Isolde are always suffering. When they finally get together, they choose to die rather than be apart. The most damning message is that Tristan and Isolde love each other more when they are isolated and suffering. From this myth has come Romeo and Juliet and all the other great romantic stories of Western literature.

In many conscious cultures there is no notion of romantic love. What we call romantic love they call spirit. It is magical and can happen between anybody. Forcing ourselves to love only one person is limiting spirit and to do that we must struggle. Passion is the form, the energy, that spirit takes on in the physical world.

Life is Not Fair – Life is filled with injustices and contradictions. This provides us with ample opportunity to play victim, blame and complain. There are no victims other than those who are ignorant or unaware of their choices. Once we are aware of our choices, we claim our rightful place as creators. The bird flies, fish swim, and humans create. Creation is our purpose. When we choose to be stuck and unhappy that is our choice, which allows us to be idle. Decisions are logical and based on the past. Choices are intuitive and throw us into the future before we are ready. When we make decisions, we are maintaining life. When we choose, we are living life.

I'm Not Good Enough – We concluded we were not good enough long before we were aware of our choices. We are all born with high self-esteem. We had no problem with being served and asked for whatever we needed. Children in toy stores don't just want a particular toy, they want the entire store. Watch adults who fear eye contact or when offered service react with "No thanks, I can do it." We were, are and always will be good enough.

As children we received attention for just being ourselves. This went on for years and then, without warning, the game changed and our mother and father became our parents. Suddenly, after years of crying to get what we needed or wanted, we are told to "Stop crying." After years of being served and cared for we were told, "Go get it yourself." The game changed and we had to perform to be good enough.

We chose to go along with the parenting game. An astute thing to do because the eight-year-old doesn't say, "I'm not willing to play your game. I'm moving out and getting my own place." In time, we forget we made the decision to survive and believed the criticism of our parents. Eventually, we conclude that our parents were right and we were wrong. Being good enough comes from being more like ourselves and not someone else. Picasso became more and more like Picasso. Einstein more and more like Einstein. Being someone else is much more difficult than being ourselves. When we are not good enough, we are usually not interested enough. The way is to choose a path of passion that leads you to excellence.

Parents are People – Parents are not people. Parenting is a job. If we are over 20 and still relate to our mother and father as parents, rather than our creators, we will always feel like a child around them. When parents believe the purpose of parenting is to make the child successful, they must pass judgment. So, every time we go home to visit our parents we will be judged. When mothers and fathers understand the purpose of parenting is to allow the child to become self-sufficient, compassion outweighs comparison and enables us to visit our creators rather than our parents.

Life Is a Struggle – Struggle is a lifelong theme for many people. It is easy to understand how we could get this idea when we realize this struggle is the foundation of most major religions. They preach how if we suffer enough here on this earthly realm after we die, they will throw a big party for us in paradise. That is a life insurance policy no one in their right mind would buy, yet most people on our planet do.

Parents complain to their children about how hard it is to be an adult and then wonder why their child doesn't want to grow up. Each night the evening news delivers horrific stories that make our day feel good by comparison to some poor person who has suffered a terrible fate. We struggle in our work, personal relationships, religion, education and health as we reward what requires effort and distrust what is easy. We work compulsively doing more and more rather than receive what's already there right in front of us.

> *"Independent has become the new word for lonely. Loneliness is an absence of self. Externals don't cause loneliness. It's not about who is gone, it's about us being present."*

I am Independent – Since our conception everyone is dependent on someone. The illusion of independence begins when our creators become parents. The parental job is to support their child in becoming self-reliant not independent. Parents know this difference. It is the child who confuses independence for self-reliance.

Rather than being unconditionally served, as a child we come to resent that we are being required to become self-reliant. Parents always want the child to visit, call or write and seldom threaten them with separation. Independent has become the new word for lonely. Loneliness is an absence of self. Externals don't cause loneliness. It's not about who is gone, it's about us being present. We can be lonely in bed next to our lover. Dependence, and more importantly interdependence, creates relationships, diminishes ego and engenders appreciation.

At first letting go of these illusions makes us unhappy because we have invested so much in them. In time we are happier because we drop the burden of independence. We discover that there is no truth, only opinion. This allows us to listen to others for the first time because we know their truth is really only their point of view and not a threat. We realize that beyond independence and dependence is interdependence, which is being self-reliant while openly appreciating those who contribute to our life.

> *"Today, when we ask a question in search of the truth, we are considered too aggressive or even hostile. It is healthy to question the truth. That is how we have achieved so much in science and art."*

Eventually we arrive at a new ease about life that is absent of judgment and our need to be right. We are willing to be ourselves and live our way. There is a feminine mythological archetype called The Questioner who, rather than nurturing, awakens us through compassionate confrontation. Today, when we ask a question in search of the truth, we are considered too aggressive or even hostile. It is healthy to question the truth. That is how we have achieved so much in science and art. We need to ask questions of ourselves like: "Why am I in this relationship? Why do I do this job? What use is all this stuff I own?" Possessions and people that we no longer value are burdens we drag around like old baggage.

Deep in the Brazilian Amazon, during an ayahuasca ritual, I was working to let go of nagging judgment. I resisted surrendering to the ritual thinking, "What am I doing in the jungle looking for answers? These people have millions of homeless children. What could they possibly know?" Then the voice of the ayahuasca spoke, "There are no homeless people in the forest." I burst out laughing at the obviousness of that statement. One truth followed another and another until I started laughing unable to recall all the truth I was being presented.

Our truth allows us to forgive, relax and let go of old baggage that's been lingering for years. When we speak our truth, our ego decreases and we accept others without anyone being wrong. Everyone wins. Our truth always puts us in present time and eliminates the upsets. To always tell the truth is not wise, but it is always to our advantage to tell ourselves the truth.

The secret is to tell ourselves the truth as fast as we can. This allows us to respond rather than react. There is integrity to the cliché, "The truth will set you free." For me, this really means our truth puts us in present time. The more we tell ourselves the truth, the more present we are. The more that we are present the more freedom we enjoy.

During this passage it is best to keep our questions simple, "How do I choose to spend my time and with whom?"

Passage 10 ~ Atonement

Healing and Forgiving the Sins of Sun and Moon

To atone we must first heal the sins of male and female. With this passage we are obliged to forgive others for their sins against us and forgive ourselves for our sins toward them. This process allows us to move beyond the manipulation of forgiveness to the wisdom of acceptance. Only then are we capable of atonement.

> *"Forgiveness is a state of consciousness, not an event or a procedure like having your tonsils removed. We are only complete in that moment of forgiving and that is why we must continue to forgive."*

My Story About Atonement

I consciously practiced forgiving for years. This requires continuous effort and I remember thinking: "How long do I have to do this? Will this ever be complete?" Years later I realized that forgiveness is forever. Forgiveness is a state of consciousness, not an event or a procedure like having your tonsils removed. We are only complete in that moment of forgiving and that is why we must continue to forgive.

My earliest understanding of forgiveness was buried under layers of Catholic dogma. Every Saturday afternoon I entered the confessional where I kneeled and confessed my sins to the parish priest. The priest would pass judgment and, beneath a statue of Jesus being crucified for my sins, I would pray to God for forgiveness. I resisted going to confession, but with time confession became an easy way for me to cleanse my conscience.

As an adult I studied the life of Christ and discovered simple things I had never considered from a different point of view. Christ was not a Christian, he was Jewish, and he rebelled against the same commerce and hypocrisy that tarnishes mainstream Christianity today. As an adult the Bible became a story of how Christ acquired and maintained an enlightened state of consciousness, a state called forgiveness.

I have had my share of people who mishandled me. A father who frightened me. A best friend who beat me because his girlfriend liked to keep him jealous. A business partner who forced my resignation by exposing details of my personal life at a time when I had sought his help. I have spent many nights tossing in my sleep dreaming of settling scores, but those dreams were always overcome with the desire to forgive.

For me forgiveness has sometimes been easy and at other times very difficult. With my mother forgiveness came easy. In the 60s I was living in Santa Monica and read Kahlil Gibran's *The Prophet*. Moved, I sent a copy to my mother in New York and asked her to read the chapter on children. After that all was forgiven between us.

With my father forgiveness took many years. One day I stole flowers from a neighbor's garden. My father caught me and insisted I put them back. "That is ridiculous," I said. "If I put them back, they will die." I watched him restrain himself. Rather than hit me, he spit in my face. I left home shortly thereafter, which began a long separation. Years later I began to visit him, arriving at his house in a chauffeured limousine, talking about my latest TV appearance. This was all about getting his approval. I still had not forgiven him.

One day I was reading a Buddha darshan diary, an entry about a man who, instead of asking Buddha a question, had spit in Buddha's face. Buddha's disciples went wild. Buddha slowly wiped his face, looked at the man and said, "Do you have anything else to say?" My father was an emotional man and not very good with words. I realized that my father's violence was all he was capable of doing. That was the way he communicated. I reached the conclusion that physical violence is the last outpost of incompetence. This began an incredible healing process between us that in time moved beyond forgiveness to atonement.

As my father got older, whenever I traveled from New York, he enjoyed picking me up at the airport. I always expressed my gratitude even though I preferred taking a taxi because he would forget where he parked the car and I would have to carry my luggage a great distance. One time, as I climbed into the front seat, my father began to cry. I reached out and held him in my arms. He wept and asked my forgiveness for being such a terrible father. "That's not true," I said. "You have been a great father, you just sucked as a parent." He laughed, wiped his eyes and we drove away. I know that as long as I live, forgiveness and atonement must be my constant companions, otherwise I risk living a life of isolation, anger and judgment.

"Atonement is deeper. It's about healing our relationship with our birth father, the world he represents and, in the process, accepting and healing the power of our denied masculine energy."

My Wisdom About Atonement

Atonement with our father is not just about the physical father. Our tendency is to focus all our distress, resentment, need for attention and complaints toward the birth father because he represents the male world with all its insensitivity and corruption. That is really why we are upset. Atonement is deeper. It's about healing our relationship with our birth father, the world he represents and, in the process, accepting and healing the power of our denied masculine energy.

The meaning of forgiveness is to give and not judge. Forgiveness practiced this way is an enlightened state of consciousness. Forgiveness that requires others to do something in order to be accepted is manipulation. Like punishment, this behavior is a penalty one has to pay to gain the favor of the forgiver.

Sincere forgiveness is always followed by joy as we dissolve the judgment and distance between us. Eventually we no longer have the need to fix others and are willing to allow them to be just the way they are. We let go of our parents and appreciate our mother and father because they gave us the greatest gift we have, the gift of our aliveness. We no longer see our children as a reflection of who we are, but instead acknowledge their unique personality.

Life has its own perfection and ease when we no longer require everything to be our way. With this ease comes curiosity and excitement as we become open to new experiences. We find pleasure and peace in others. Healing our masculine energy comes with the willingness to love, which is being conscious of what we value about that person. To heal ourselves we must first forgive our relationships and that creates the opportunity for them to heal us.

We feel betrayed by those we liked, trusted and loved. Beneath our resentment and pain is the desire that our expectations of them had been fulfilled. Unfortunately, with some people forgiveness remains only a dream.

Forgiveness is to give up resentment or the desire to punish someone, to stop being angry and to give up power and control.

Atonement is to allow yourself to just be and to receive. By so doing you allow others to be the way they are and to discover the true value of that experience.

Passage 11 ~ Spiritual Elderhood

Mistress/Master of Many Worlds

The Fourth Triad: Realization

Spiritual Elderhood begins the Fourth Triad: Realization, that includes Passage 12 ~ Sharing Your Wisdom, and Passage 13 ~ Beyond Duality. This triad takes us through the transformation of death to our reincarnation.

My Story About Spiritual Elderhood

I was born with congenital cataracts and diagnosed industrially blind. Reading was tedious and slow causing me to seek out teachers with whom to apprentice rather than just read their books. For a long time, I felt victimized by this until I realized how fortunate I was to hear their genius first hand. A few of these teachers were extraordinary like Michael Hughes, who fathered me into the realm of the occult, to Chuck Dederich who was the first to hammer on my rock. The courageously wild intelligence of Osho challenged my truth and Baba Muktananda who opened my heart.

Michael possessed many powers. He channeled and spoke in tongues, invoked and manifested entities, predicted my future with incredible accuracy. When he laid on hands, darkness left my body and was immediately replaced by a tingling light sensation. After one of Michael's light session my girlfriend remarked how I was different and much more relaxed, how I spoke from a higher consciousness and appeared younger and more vibrant. When I questioned the accuracy of her observations, she insisted I sit down so she could take a few Polaroids so I could see the difference.

The first image revealed only a faint image of my presence, which we dismissed as poor photography or bad film. She took another. In the second image there was only an unfocused outline of me. Everything else was in focus including the indentation my body made in the leather sofa. More images yielded similar results. She freaked out and threw the camera on the floor. "You're not here," she whispered. We looked at each other in disbelief, laughed and mimicked sounds from *The Twilight Zone*. We were never able to repeat the experience, but we had the Polaroids to show the skeptics.

Michael gave me an old book *The Song of Sano Tarot*. I took it home and avoided reading it for weeks. One Saturday, without a thought, I reached for the book, opened to a random page and started reading. As I read a strong voice from deep inside of me started reading aloud. I stood up and loudly preached the words until I was yelling. Suddenly, I became aware of what I was doing. Frightened, I dropped the book on the floor and called Michael. He answered the phone saying, "So, you read the book."

Michael lived in a weird old mansion in Beverly Hills with underground passages. The master bedroom was fifty feet long with a stage at one end. The living room was so large and light that you felt like you were outside. The garden was tropical with huge statues of Buddha, Gods and Goddesses. There was a waterfall that flowed down a lava rock wall covered with orchids. I wanted to ask Michael why he lived in such a house but never did. There were stories around Michael about this house and how he made money. One day he was complaining about the expense of the orchids. I asked and he explained his business was real estate, that the house was so weird and expensive it was seldom rented so he lived there during those down times.

That afternoon Michael shared that whenever he needed money, he would do real estate deals and that today was one of those times.

We climbed into his Cadillac Eldorado convertible and drove around Beverly Hills. Occasionally, he would stop in front of a house, close his eyes, and mumble in tongues. He'd drive away until he was moved to stop in front of another house and repeat the ritual. "What are you doing?" I asked. "Reading the people in these houses," he said. "To see if they are happy or thinking of selling." After a few hours we went home. With the advantage of his channeled information, he got on the phone wheeling and dealing. Two days later he closed a deal for a $130,000 commission.

I discovered Baba Muktananda in an occult bookstore in New York when I was looking for something esoteric and easy to read. *Getting Rid of What You Haven't Got* was a thin book with Muktananda's head shot on the back cover. That evening I noticed the eyes in Muktananda's photo following me. At first, I was freaked out then started laughing as his eyes followed me around the room. The next day a friend told me that Baba was in nearby South Fallsburg, New York. Later I learned synchronicities were common around Muktananda. I immediately wrote and asked if we could meet.

His translator Malti, now Guru Mai, invited me to South Fallsburg that weekend. Unaware of the significance of this invitation I had to postpone because of a speaking engagement in Pittsburgh that same weekend. During my lecture in Pittsburgh a voice came into my head, over and over, "Baba, Baba, Baba." It was Muktananda. This voice made it impossible for me to focus on what I was saying. I put the audience into a guided meditation, asked my assistant to take charge and left for New York.

My driver Carlton picked me up at the airport and we headed to Muktananda's ashram. When we arrived Malti came down the steps of the main building and said, "Mr. Natale, Baba is very pleased that you are here." I turned to Carlton, "Did you call to say we were coming?" He shook his head.

"Then another voice said, 'Are you crazy, you know this man ten minutes and already you want to do his magic.' So, I continued with the self-conscious social niceties, thanked him and announced I had to leave."

Once in Baba's presence I kneeled and he struck me over the head with a large wand of peacock feathers. Suddenly my brain went clear and I forgot all of the significant questions I had been preparing since Pittsburgh. I pretended to not be foolish and started talking about trivia. All the time this voice in my head kept saying, "Ask Baba to teach you how to initiate Shaktipat." Later I learned this is the transmission of spiritual energy from one person to another, either through touch or an object like a peacock wand. This was outrageous because I had no memory of ever hearing the word Shaktipat. Then another voice said, "Are you crazy, you know this man ten minutes and already you want to do his magic." So, I continued with the self-conscious social niceties, thanked him and announced I had to leave.

Baba struck me on the head with his peacock wand seven more times. As I stood to leave Baba whispered to Malti in Hindi. She said, "Baba says for you to come back seven more times and you will know how to initiate Shaktipat." I flew out of Baba's room and up the stairs, people smiling at me all the way. When I reached my room, Carlton went on about how wonderful the ashram was. I told him we were leaving, picked up my bag and headed for the door. Carlton laughed. "What's so funny?" I asked. And he said, "You don't have any shoes." I laughed and, with complete humility, went back down to retrieve my shoes. I returned to Baba's ashram countless times.

On Muktananda's birthday I took my five-year-old son Jason. We arrived too late to enter the meditation hall so Jason and I sat waiting for the ceremony to finish. Right after the applause Baba was first out of the doors. He came over to us and smiled, touched both of us on the head and walked toward his quarters. Later I was telling a friend about how fortunate we were to meet Baba. "You're crazy," he said. "Baba went out the usual way behind his chair, not the main doors." In disbelief I asked Jason, "Did you see daddy's friend the saint (that's what Jason called Muktananda)?" He replied, "Yes, I saw him." Then he motioned with his hand toward his head. These materializations and dematerializations were common around Muktananda, but his greatest miracle was the security, love and joy that permeated his ashram community.

"Absent of their cultural conditioning elders see magic in the obvious and relate to the essence of each individual, not just their personality. Elders reclaim their power and the safety of infancy as they travel the inner landscape of their mind."

My Wisdom About Elderhood

An Elder is one who has realized their potential and self-actualized. They are teachers, gurus, shaman, wise old crones, grandmothers and grandfathers. Absent of their cultural conditioning elders see magic in the obvious and relate to the essence of each individual, not just their personality. Elders reclaim their power and the safety of infancy as they travel the inner landscape of their mind. Elders have a sense of humor about life and possess many answers to the same question.

Elders possess an expanded perception of reality. They accept and are at peace with themselves and others. Elders are spontaneous in their thinking and emotional expression. They're not a problem to themselves and thus can focus elsewhere. Elders enjoy time alone and exhibit a high degree of autonomy. They're creative, have a sense of humor and openly express their gratitude. Elders have impressive ethics and prefer to expose the dishonest. They resist the brainwashing and cultural imprinting. Elders have integrated their male and female energy. Elders can hold more than one point of view at a time. They know it's not your problem that must transform, but your point of view. What elders do best is travel to parallel realities; they are Mistress/Master of many worlds.

The World of the Physical – Elders spend most of their time in the physical world. Earth is our home, the reality that created us. Once a student asked, "What's a Wizard?" And I answered, "I can't tell you what we are, only what we do. When God and Goddess created the Earth, everything was perfect and in peace and harmony. God and Goddess became bored with perfection and created Wizards to play with reality." The lesson here is that life is the only game there is and our gift is to play and enjoy it.

> *"Elders know what the novice misses: to witness and be present in the world of the mundane. This empowers us to have the problem and objectively witness it at the same time. This provides the distance to understand, which is essential for healing."*

The World of the Mundane – The mundane is so similar to the physical world that many novices miss its value and complain "nothing happened" or "I didn't experience anything." It is here that the answers to the problems of everyday life reside. Elders know what the novice misses: to witness and be present in the world of the mundane. This empowers us to have the problem and objectively witness it at the same time. This provides the distance to understand, which is essential for healing. The lesson here is that problems are often an outcome of our environment. In order to heal them we must briefly distance ourselves from that environment and return with a renewed perception that is willing and capable of healing.

The World of the Surreal – In this world we may find ourselves dancing with a giant serpent. With the exception of us this world is composed of surrealistic forms. Once we begin to interpret the experience rather than fear the experience, we learn to read and understand the meaning of color, movement, form and other symbols of our collective unconscious. The lesson here is that when we avoid our fears and turn our backs, fear becomes more powerful. When we look at our fears they dissolve in understanding and transform into our alert guardians.

The World of Wonder – Here we are thrown into a world beyond our control. We are absent of will and can only return to reality after the experience has run its course. Once during an Amazonian ayahuasca ritual I drifted into a trance and found myself in "The World of Plants." I was forced to drop my control and interact with wonder. Everything was telepathic and communication occurred through focused thought alone. Branches of trees embraced me. Incredible eyes smiled from the huge root systems of the trees. Everything was alive. I touched one tree and was stuck with the needle of a cactus, but this tree was not a cactus. I touched it and was stuck again. In disbelief I foolishly touched it and was stuck once again. In anger I said, "What are you doing?" The tree said, "Don't touch me." The next morning, I went back into the jungle looking for that tree, but found nothing. The lesson is that when we drop our need to control and move beyond our fear, we discover wonder and appreciate all the aliveness that surrounds us.

The World of Light – I have only gone here once. In this world it's all light and no form; we exist only as thought. I realized this is death and, in a panic, struggled to return to normal reality. When I returned, I had a renewed appreciation for the physical world. Earth is home. The reason I spend so much time here is that I love it. After this experience I saw the wonder of Earth as I did as a child. Suddenly, everything was a miracle, a place I feel comfortable, yet do not totally understand. The lesson is that enlightened consciousness will come on its own after many deaths, perceived or actual, and that we must leave our physical reality once in a while to truly appreciate it.

Elders come from a place of compassion and service. Compassion is understanding and accepting another person's contribution, to receive their experience without judgment. Compassion is what creates miracles in people.

Service is giving assistance absent of expectation. Service is about taking care of someone beyond reason. Service is knowing somebody and handling his or her need rather than what we need.

REALIZATION (52+ years)

Passage 12 ~ Sharing Your Wisdom

Return to Family, Friends and Community

My Story About Sharing

By the time I was a young boy I had lost my self-esteem. Once your self-esteem is gone, sharing becomes impossible. I had almost no confidence and survived under the shield of my rebelliousness. Eventually I learned we are all born with high self-esteem, that all the damage was inflicted along the way. My poor eyesight, dysfunctional family and the rough streets of Brooklyn can be credited with the systematic undermining of my self-esteem. Ultimately the reclaiming of my self-esteem, my worthiness, must be credited to my friends, students and colleagues that showered me with abundance and appreciation. I also express gratitude for the great teachers in my life. Their wisdom and demonstration kept me on track through the most difficult times.

My mother taught me how to love unconditionally. My father modeled strong work ethics. Chuck Dederich was among the first to acknowledge my talents and give me the courage to use them. Michael taught me how to acknowledge and engage powers beyond my understanding. Baba Muktananda taught me that everything was my creation, and to only receive gifts.

Baba had a commercial stand outside of his meditation hall where visitors could buy him a gift before asking a question at darshan. If you purchased a gift with great significance, he would pass it off to one of his disciples who would run back outside and return it for resale. Baba would pass on a Rolex watch and keep a piece of fruit. He did this playfully, laughing while saying in Hindi, "Only gifts, never bribes." The message was clear, but it took me a while to manifest this integrity. My realization of Baba's many messages continues to this day.

"As a teacher I was expected to demonstrate my capacity for sharing. It is a tradition to pass on what has been given, however, you have little to share unless you are capable of receiving."

The hostile environment of my youth caused me to shut down. My willingness to share emerged when I recognized and addressed my inability to receive. Because of my poor and sickly early life my need to invest in scarcity was one of the most difficult areas of my life to transform. I struggled to say "yes" and "thank you." This may sound silly because it's so simple. Now when someone asks if I need help, I say yes. Before I would say, "No thank you I'll manage it myself." Then I'd withdraw to suffer in private. Since Synanon and Phoenix House to Actualizations and The Natale Institute, I have always shared because that's a major part of my work. As a teacher I was expected to demonstrate my capacity for sharing. It is a tradition to pass on what has been given, however, you have little to share unless you are capable of receiving.

In the early 70s I was introduced to the commercial marketing power and effectiveness of sharing during my involvement with EST (Erhard Seminar Training). The large EST trainings, with their sales teams and product offerings, demonstrated how I did and did not want to share in my work. In the 80s I created a balanced approach working with students in workshops and making it possible for them to license and present my courses. Friends like Neil Diamond and Ben Gazzara encouraged me to share and become more visible by writing books and producing music. Once in the recording studio Neil said, "Frankie you should write a book. People should know what you have to say."

In 1970 I was 29 years old, director of Phoenix House helping addicts overcome chemical dependency, appeared frequently on radio and TV, and wrote guest editorials about our work for *The New York Times* and the *New York Daily News*. I wrote the article "A Celebration of Life" for *Mademoiselle* magazine about the power of sharing in our lives and in recovery: "Our program has to do with people celebrating life, celebrating themselves, their bodies and their minds, and teaching people that they don't need chemicals to enjoy life. You can call it drug rehabilitation if you want, but that's crazy. It's just getting the individual into himself."

> *"Sharing dissolves our feelings of separateness. Sharing is what gives our relationships their true value. The act of sharing transforms our relationships and it transforms us."*

My Wisdom About Sharing

Be aware that our reasons for sharing will change, otherwise we risk feeling like a victim who is giving more than they are receiving. Sharing dissolves our feelings of separateness. Sharing is what gives our relationships their true value. The act of sharing transforms our relationships and it transforms us. Sharing is an opportunity to give, encourage, assist, nourish and acknowledge. Sharing brings experience into being. Sharing clears up misunderstandings, conflicts and resentments.

When we consciously share, we contribute to the lives of others and therefore ourselves. We nourish and share what we have, knowing there is great abundance. We are willing to share because we know what we share has been shared with us. We communicate our gratitude to those who contribute to our life. We express our intention and are willing to create.

Passage 13 ~ Beyond Duality

Death, the Final Passage

My Story About Duality

Until recently, as I approach my final passage, I preferred to live on the edge of reality and that has often brought me close to death. Once in Guatemala my guide took me deep into the rainforest. Suddenly, he froze and motioned for me to be still. The guide's face went white. There was a jaguar. I froze, terrified that I was about to be an animal's lunch. The jaguar looked at us, licked its lips and kept moving. For a long minute I thought my time had come. Later the guide explained we were lucky that the jaguar was not hungry. We had no weapons. There was nowhere to run. Since that experience, and others like it, I no longer needed to venture into the wild. It's easy for city dwellers watching television to want to save wild beasts from extinction, a sentiment with which I totally agree. When you're facing death in the wild, however, you gain a unique perspective.

> *"When we lived closer to nature, winter was considered the season of death. Winter was a time to go inside and search our souls in preparation for the re-birth of spring."*

In the natural wilderness death is everywhere, yet we are a culture who moves away from our natural state. When we lived closer to nature, winter was considered the season of death. Winter was a time to go inside and search our souls in preparation for the rebirth of spring. One Christmas holiday I invited a group of Amazonian friends to my home in Amsterdam. Some had never traveled outside of the Amazon jungle. As we came out of Schiphol airport one of them pointed to a tree and said, "Frank, why have your trees died?" She had never seen dormant trees without leaves. For her the trees were dead. That was when I accepted death from a fresh perspective and likened it to a winter sleep. The passage of winter was a time to go home, not to escape the cold, but to let go of a busy brain and weary body. We can be certain, similar to the passing of seasons, that our transformation, our reincarnation will arrive like springtime. Death is just a part of what we call life.

As a teacher I have been privileged with the opportunity to support people preparing for the final passage. This has always been a sad experience, but the mystery of death continues to fascinate me. Death is like going on an adventure unaware of the destination. What is horrifying to me is that too many of us die in pain and most of this pain could be eliminated.

As he was dying my father was in a lot of pain. Each time I asked the hospital staff to ease the pain another family member would resist because the pain confirmed that death was eminent. These selfish interventions infuriated me. Only months before my father was an active muscular man. Now his legs had shriveled to the size of my wrists. It was obvious that his time to die had come. At the moment of death my father became calm, his energy released and left the body. I could feel this and, to my amazement, some of his energy entered my body. This confirmed what I had always suspected, that separation exists as form alone. At the level of our spirit, at the level of our soul, we are one. The experience of my father's passing was beautiful and uplifting. I sat there for twenty minutes knowing my father was still within me.

"In the Results Course we teach that fish swim, birds fly, and humans create. Our miraculous power to manifest reality goes virtually unnoticed. This power is taken for granted because we are always in the reality we created."

In our Western culture we think it is somehow wise to protect children from mourning the death of a relative. Death is an important event in their life, especially if they had a close connection. I lived with a large extended family. There were cousins and other family to play with, but Aunt Betty was my favorite. Aunt Betty was bedridden yet always happy to see me and share her wonderful stories. One day after school I rushed to Aunt Betty's room, but she was not there. This was a shock because she was always there. I asked my mother and was told, "She's gone and will not be coming back." Without explanation, I watched family members pack Aunt Betty's belongings, crying and speaking in whispers. I was very sad for months afterward.

It was not until adulthood that I realized Aunt Betty had always been there for me because she was an invalid and unable to move. I never completed with her. For many years afterward I rebelled when faced with death in any form. When my mother died, I flew to New York to attend her funeral only to find a closed casket. My turn came to pay my respect. I kneeled before the casket then opened it and placed peacock feathers and a photo of Baba inside to accompany my mother on her passage. The family was outraged.

My illness began in 1995. By 1998 I entered a long ride through what I call "nightmare alley." After years of thinking I would recover, I nearly died in Amsterdam and was forced to leave Europe for the medical care needed to stay alive. Back in the States I did what had worked in the past, I went into the Southern Arizona desert for a 21-day water fast. This time my condition worsened. My belly and legs swelled with huge amounts of retained water. My dear friend Ayman Sawaf came and took me to his home in Marin, California. There in the hospital I was diagnosed with diabetes, hepatitis-C, cirrhosis, end stage kidney disease, and anemia caused by internal bleeding. I was dying, homeless, and felt totally alone.

The nightmare that followed included many near-death experiences while in my bed, in emergency rooms, and intensive care units. Now, I regularly enter the hospital to receive dialysis. Over the last few years, thanks to doctors, friends and family, I have learned to cope with my illness and have created a new and rewarding life. There were times going through this nightmare I was ready to die, complete about how I had lived. Then one day I realized there was nothing special about dying. I could die any time. The challenge was to reinvent myself, be creative and enjoy the life I had. My situation stabilized. I thought that death itself was less frightening than the painful process of how I was dying. Again, I'm alive and eternally grateful for each joyous moment knowing death could easily come at any moment.

In the Results Course we teach that fish swim, birds fly, and humans create. Our miraculous power to manifest reality goes virtually unnoticed. This power is taken for granted because we are always in the reality we created. Think about a fish, it doesn't know that it lives in water until it finds itself on the shore. Human beings can visualize and create our day-to-day future within the context of this life. So, I think we should be able to visualize and manifest our next life. In the past I have attempted to do this, but only vague images came to me.

As I grew older and closer to death the ability to envision and manifest my next life eventually appeared. My dreams are clear and instructive. I am presented with choices like: "Would you prefer to reincarnate into a species at the height of their evolution that possess telepathic powers and abilities that defy physics?" or "Would you prefer a species that is still evolving and filled with opportunities, choices and adventure?" My dreams reveal the unexplainable conditions of my life. Why did I meet Ichiko in Europe, who suddenly appeared like an angel whose care and willingness to stand by me literally saved my life? Who was she and why was she with me? Why did I grow to love her more than I've loved any woman? Why did we choose to marry knowing that I may die soon?

My dreams revealed the shape of a divine plan: Ichiko was my companion who would bring me through this life and into the next. My work had been in North and South America, Europe and Africa. My next life would be in Asia. This dream came to me on Ichiko's 30th birthday. I awoke with a great feeling of peace, eager to share this clarity with Ichiko. Ironically, when we met in Europe years earlier, she wanted to learn more about past lives. My chaos and questions were replaced with purpose and direction. This teaching dream served as spiritual confirmation of the fourth triad of realization, the period that brings us through the death/life process into the early stages of the next. I had written about this a year before I received that dream.

"When we are willing to see it, death is everywhere as part of the natural cycle of everything. Most of us live in denial of our death because to accept it would radically change the way we live."

My Wisdom About Duality

Death moves us beyond the physical world of duality. Like death, each night when we dream, we move into this same world of non-duality. When we are willing to see it, death is everywhere as part of the natural cycle of everything. Most of us live in denial of our death because to accept it would radically change the way we live. We pretend we're not getting older and that makes preparing for death impossible. Aging and dying has become un-American. In the past our elderly were cared for by loved ones and died in their own home with their family and friends present.

Dealing with death can be sterile and avoided. We can hire someone to come and get the body, embalm it so it looks alive, put it in a closed coffin or have it cremated. We don't have to touch, see or ever go near the body again. We make the choice to either have a hands-on funeral or distance ourselves from the whole experience. It's not about right or wrong. This is about making the choice that is best for us. I have seldom felt the need to grieve and rarely attended funeral death rituals because to grieve a lifeless body seemed foolish. How to deal with death has always been a choice. The Kalahari Bushman, a 40,000-year-old culture, grieve and bury their dead where they lived. They move their entire village and do not return until enough generations have passed for the death to be forgotten.

> "People fear death because they fear they have not lived enough. This fear takes on new meaning once we realize our fear of death is equivalent to our fear of living."

Even if we believe in reincarnation, when death comes, we are sad because we won't be able to enjoy the physical presence of that person. One of the saddest funerals I experienced was that of Osho Rajneesh. Many of his followers believed it was unenlightened to express grief so the sannyasis attempted to withhold their sorrow as they danced and celebrated half-heartedly. I became sad, not for the memory of Osho, but for his disciples who, after all of Osho's lectures about death, were clearly in denial. People fear death because they fear they have not lived enough. This fear takes on new meaning once we realize our fear of death is equivalent to our fear of living.

Long after the death of my mother and father I would speak with them, either in my dreams or while engaged in some activity we had shared. For my mother, it was when I cooked. My father would communicate with me in the morning while I shaved. I saw him reflected in the mirror in my eyes. It's possible to channel loved ones and communicate with the deceased. Their bodies are dead but their spirit lives on as thought.

When a close friend's son committed suicide people told him,

"Let go, move on, come to peace with his passing." My friend was profoundly depressed with such serious chest pains he thought he was having a heart attack. He asked for my advice. "The chest pain is you holding on to your son," I said. "This is how you keep him around. You should never get over it. Instead embrace these feelings as your son's physical presence." He burst into tears and cried for over an hour. When the tears had run their course the chest pains faded and morphed into a soft feeling of his son's presence that nurtured him.

> *"A secret to living life fully is to be present,*
> *to live in each moment and, importantly,*
> *allow our judgments to die in each moment.*
> *To live fully is to live without expectation."*

Much has been written about death. When I look at death all I see is life. The consideration of death is an incredible experience that reveals an objective review of our life. Death serves as a great alarm clock, a wake-up call reminding us to realize what we value and to communicate our appreciation to loved ones. In the West we tend to think of death as the final linear conclusion, but many cultures believe in the immortality cycle of death and resurrection. Wherever there is death there is birth. A secret to living life fully is to be present, to live in each moment and, importantly, allow our judgments to die in each moment. To live fully is to live without expectation. To stop withholding and be complete with everyone is to be ready whenever should death come. Everything dies and is eventually resurrected. This is a path that Eastern mystics have described for ages.

Very few elders today choose how, where and when they will die. This choice is given to our doctors and family with the most popular way to die is from a debilitating disease in a hospital or nursing home. Our early ancestors would go to a high mountain cliff, declare their last testament and jump to their death. They believed, as we do in our dreams, they would leave their body before they hit the ground. As we get older, for the first time, there are reasons for death. Our body is tired or broken, we have completed all we felt a passion to accomplish. Most of our loved ones have passed and we miss them. These reasons replace the physical immortality we naively believed during our youth.

If we have lived consciously, we will die consciously. Many people have hearts that beat. They breathe, but they are dead. They are unconscious. Conscious death is about accepting the inevitability of death and preparing for it. It's about completing relationships and putting our life in order so we may relax and enjoy the rest of our life.

Here are a few examples of those who died consciously: the humble parting of spiritual teacher George Gurdjieff and the spectacular death ritual of Paramahansa Yogananda. Toward the end of his life Gurdjieff was restricted to bed and unable to move. One evening he told his doctor, "Call the ambulance. It's time." His doctor left the room and made the call. When he returned, to his surprise, Gurdjieff was missing. He was not in bed and not in the house. The doctor found Gurdjieff standing in the street waiting for the ambulance smoking a cigar, wearing his long underwear and favorite hat.

Yogananda rented the large ballroom of the Roosevelt Hotel in Los Angeles, sent hundreds of invitations to his disciples and, at the appropriate moment, laid down on an alter and left his body. On the last pages of the classic book *Autobiography of a Yogi* they reference Yogananda's autopsy, which stated that for two weeks after death his body showed no signs of cellular decomposition.

My grandmother requested the entire family fly in from all over the world. She died within one day of everyone's arrival. There are a few things we can do to learn to die consciously. Look at death. Do not look away. Do not avoid it because death is everywhere. Spend time and sit with a dying person. Hold their hand, hold them in your arms, feel their energy. Invite loved ones who have died to visit you in your dreams. Make your end-of-life wishes known and commit them to legal documents. Do you have an advance directive and will? Should you be incapacitated, how do you want to be cared for? Do you prefer being buried or cremated? Who will receive your physical possessions?

Imagine your life will be over in a month. What would you do differently? What relationships and tasks require completion? Who would you call to acknowledge and say goodbye? Imagine your life after death and create, in detail, your next life. Will you manifest an entirely new environment or will you return to your present reality? Who in your life now do you want to meet again in your next life?

In ancient Greece the average life expectancy was 20 years. During the Middle Ages, if you survived the plague, war, and starvation, the average life was 30 years. Another 600 years passed before life expectancy reached 37 years. Those born around 1900 could expect to live to age 50. Now, in less than a century, we can expect to live 75 or more years. Significantly longer lives can be expected in the future. By 2025 the United States will have an estimated 50 million people over 65 years old, our longevity attributed to the control of major disease, improved diet and physical fitness.

> *"We are truly living The Circle of Life*
> *when we have planned for the final passage,*
> *when we have prepared to return our bodies*
> *to the elements and set our souls free beyond*
> *the limitations of the physical world."*

Looking at our death is a valuable way to examine our lives as a reflection of our life and a reminder of the inevitable. Accepting that after death we live on as consciousness does not make death any easier. We are saddened by the loss of our loved ones, however, an important task of elderhood is to prepare for death. Creating rituals helps accomplish this. Our ancestors made death masks, envisioned their next life, gave living testimony and prepared where and how they would die.

One of my favorite death rituals is from Korea where the shaman are women called mudangs. When someone dies the mudangs come to your house and question you about all of your possessions. If a photograph, piece of furniture or other possession is related to the person who died, and has no relevance in your present life, they throw it away. They literally do spiritual house cleaning. If you resist, they playfully bump you on the head with a dead fish.

The vision for my final days is to be surrounded by loved ones and celebrate the extraordinary gift of life we have shared. This idyllic scene is desired by many, yet experienced by few. Many of us die suddenly, others sedated in the sterile confines of a hospital. Those scenarios are unfortunate because, as we approach the final passage, it is powerful to acknowledge the love and support of our family, friends and associates, and to become complete with as many relationships as possible. I have always loved being in nature, savoring the awareness found with the warmth of the sun and the wind on my face. We are truly living The Circle of Life when we have planned for the final passage, when we have prepared to return our bodies to the elements and set our souls free beyond the limitations of the physical world.

Every challenge is an opportunity to move past the "vicious circle of change" and reclaim our remarkable power to create and transform. As you travel The Circle of Life, embrace your magic and a new world of possibilities. That is the way to go.

– With love and light,

Explore the Self-Discovery pages with healing visualizations and rites of passage experiences.

Epilogue

Early in June of 2002 Frank called to say goodbye. I was well aware of his illness. The year before I had visited him in Northern California. That day he was bedridden with a dozen amber prescription bottles, illuminated by the afternoon sun, neatly aligned on the windowsill. He was optimistic about his recovery and work, including *The Circle of Life* manuscript, and returning to teach in Europe. When his health did not improve, Frank moved to Hawaii.

"Goodbye? Now where are you going?"

"The great adventure," Frank said. "The final passage. I'm going into hospice care. The plan is to leave on my birthday, after sunset."

I promised I would be there. In Honolulu a group of friends gathered at Frank's apartment from as far as Europe and Australia. Frank loved to celebrate his birthday, the longest day of the year, with a festival of light. The first few days of that week were busy as friends phoned from around the world. One afternoon we drove along the coast past Diamond Head so Frank could gaze at the Pacific Ocean for the last time. We tended to Frank and took turns sitting with him in a bedroom that overlooked a wide canal and lush green hills that rolled off to the north.

We prepared communal meals, played music and spoke quietly about our experiences with Frank. Knowing how he loved Mexican food, I made a large batch of guacamole molded into the shape of a fish with tortilla chips for fins and invited the group to the bedroom.

"Oh no," Frank said. "What's this?"

"Guacamole dip," I offered. "You have the honor of the first taste."

"What are you trying to do," Frank moaned. "Kill me?"

Everyone laughed. Frank smiled, took one taste and then another. The Europeans loved the guacamole and we used his bed as a serving table. Over the next few days Frank and I discussed his work and the gratitude and love we shared. Everyone had their time. Frank soon fell into a coma-like state, his breathing faint but steady. The final afternoon a storm brought heavy rain that moved quickly over the hills followed by a bright sun and clear blue skies.

Late that evening Frank called out "stop" and took his last breath. Ichiko and Frank's son Jason and the rest of us wept and prayed and offered our farewells. A bittersweet experience, but Frank had the final passage he envisioned. It was a profound and beautiful moment.

Namaste,

Ralph

About Frank Natale

A teacher and author, Frank Natale was founder and creative director of The Natale Institute and Frank Natale & Associates, experiential
education organizations presenting seminars and programs throughout
the United States, Europe and Australia. Natale's teaching emphasized
self-discovery, personal responsibility and choice as paths to conscious
living and spiritual growth.

Experiential seminars created by Frank Natale include Trance
Dance, the dance of life; Rites of Passage, exploring life's inevitable
transformations; The One Experience; Alive Relationships; Results, a
course in creative consciousness; Creative Communications, the experience of being understood; and Self Esteem, the power within.

Committed to dance as a healing force, Natale, with his band

Professor Trance, produced a body of music featuring extended play tracks including the albums Shaman's Breath, Medicine Trance, Rites of Passage, Dance Your Animal, Dancers of Eternity, Spirit Animal and Breath of Fire.

Books by Frank Natale include *The Circle of Life*; *Relationships for Life; Results: The Willingness to Create*; *The Wisdom of Midlife;* and *Trance Dance, the Dance of Life.*

A native New Yorker, in 1967 Natale co-founded Phoenix House in New York, which became the largest residential treatment facility for chemical dependency in the United States. After serving as clinical director for twelve years, Natale chose to leave Phoenix House and focus his work on successful, functioning personalities who want to experience new levels of spirituality, creativity and aliveness.

During the Sixties and Seventies Natale studied and worked with many leaders of the modern human consciousness movement including Charles Dederich, Abraham Maslow, Carl Rogers, Fritz Perls, Baba Muktananda, J. Krishnamurti and Buckminster Fuller.

Natale passed in June, 2002 in Hawaii surrounded by family and friends.

For more, visit FrankNatale.com

Self-Discovery

Meditation and trance music by Frank Natale or Frank Natale & Professor Trance is available for download on most digital music platforms. The self-discovery experiences on the following pages reference specific tracks from these albums:

- Om (bilateral alignment)
- Ambient Om
- Rites of Passage
- Shamanic Journey
- Medicine Trance

Self-discovery ritual experiences are presented for each of *The Circle of Life* passages. Some of these rituals may be experienced alone, others are designed for a group setting, and some are to be shared with a partner. If working with a partner, choose someone that you trust will fully participate so you may support each other and share a meaningful experience. You may want to have a pen and journal on hand to record your thoughts and responses.

Most of these experiences, including the trance dances, involve breath patterns to open our hearts and expand our consciousness in constructive ways. Approach them with a sense of reverence and wonder as they have been presented countless times through the years in our Natale workshops. If you choose to facilitate any of these in a group setting, be sure to understand the process clearly, have the music ready and commit to supporting everyone's experience. The e-book *Natale Trance Dance* is a helpful guide for presenters to stage successful events.

Passage 1 ~ Birth

Ritual: The Immortal Breath
Music: Natale Om

Find a quiet place where you can lie comfortably on your back without being disturbed. Play the Natale OM track for 20 to 60 minutes. If you have never practiced this Taoist breath pattern, begin with 20 minutes.

Remove jewelry and anything that may become a distraction. Lie quietly with your legs uncrossed, hands and arms away from the body.

Experience: Begin to inhale fully yet gently through the nose and exhale through your mouth in a circular manner. Do not cut off or hold your breath. At some point your breath will take over, the pattern will develop its own rhythm. In time this breath pattern will alter your consciousness and take you to places not accessible in normal consciousness.

The states of consciousness you experience are strongly related to your breath and therefore your birth. If you are reluctant to breathe fully, relax and keep breathing. Bring the breath to your chest. Should you become fearful, pause and breathe normally through the nose. Resume the breath when you feel comfortable. Be aware you may be relaxed and tempted to fall asleep. Stay with it.

Once you have completed twenty minutes of these breath cycles you will emerge from this state relaxed and euphoric. With completion of thirty to sixty minutes you may experience the magical vision of your immortality.

Ritual: Trance Dance
Music: Rites of Passage, "Dance the Day Away"

Find a quiet place where you won't be disturbed. Stand relaxed and ground your feet. Begin the breath of fire: two quick inhales through the nose and one exhale through the mouth. Play the music. Close your eyes and/or wear a blindfold. Move with the rhythm.

Experience: Visualize your heart beating; mother and child; the gifts of beauty, joy and protection; guardian angels; spirit animals; children dancing; a birthday party; smiling faces of infants and children. If you choose, continue listening to the next track. When complete, open your eyes and recount your visions.

Passage 2 ~ Coming of Age

Ritual: Soul Hunt
Music: Shamanic Journey

The purpose of this ritual is to travel beyond space and time and retrieve soul parts lost when, during coming of age, we denied our inner "teenage friend" (yourself at that age). Play the Natale "Shamanic Journey" track.

Experience: Find a quiet place where you can lie down for at least 30 minutes without being disturbed. Lie on your back with your feet, legs, arms and hands uncrossed and away from your body. Bring awareness to your breath. Breathe simply and deeply, in and out. Become more relaxed on each exhale.

Play the music. Close your eyes and/or wear a blindfold. Be clear about your intention to meet your inner teenage self so you may restore and bring back their power. Embrace the experience of being present with your teenage self and accepting them just the way they are. Be aware and heal as many of the traumas as you can. Become whole and complete.

When the drumming stops, slowly bring yourself back to normal consciousness. Be sure to acknowledge the return of this lost aspect of yourself. Speak to it, touch your heart or another part of your body where you now feel its presence most strongly. Play their favorite music and dance.

Ritual: Trance Dance
Music: Rites of Passage, "Young Rebel"

Find a quiet place where you won't be disturbed. Stand relaxed and ground your feet. Begin the breath of fire technique: two quick inhales through the nose and one exhale through the mouth. Play the music. Close your eyes and/or wear a blindfold. Move with the rhythm.

Experience: Visualize isolation; teenage boys and girls; the number 13; early life confrontations; teenage awkwardness; fear and anger; sadness; adventure; joy, laughter and loss of control. If you choose, continue listening to the next track. When complete, open your eyes and recount your visions.

Passage 3 ~ Separation from the Feminine

Ritual: Denied Feminine
Music: Natale Om

This is a group experience. Participants sit in a circle. You will need a symbolic element, a crystal or a stone, to pass around. Play the Om music softly so those sharing may be heard.

Experience: The person facilitating the group invites everyone to share their thoughts and feelings about the ways they separated from their mother and have denied their feminine nature. As example, the leader holds the stone, shares their experience then passes the stone to the left. Only those willing to share may hold the stone. Those who are unwilling to share pass the stone. When the stone has completed the circle, the ritual is complete. A discussion following the ritual is helpful to bring awareness to the experience and acknowledge the participants.

An alternative with eight or more participants:

Create a man's circle and a woman's circle, gathering separately for 20 to 45 minutes, depending on the number of participants. The separate groups share the ways they separated from the feminine during their teenage "Coming of Age" passage. Next, form one large circle. The facilitator invites participants, in a receptive manner, to gaze slowly into the eyes of as many others in the circle as possible. The facilitator holds the stone, shares about their feminine nature and passes the stone to the left as described above.

Ritual: Trance Dance
Music: Rites of Passage, "A Time for Separation"

You may dance as a group after sharing (or alone). If in a group, the facilitator will explain the process. Stand relaxed and ground your feet. Begin the breath of fire: two quick inhales through the nose and one exhale through the mouth. Play the music. Close your eyes and/or wear a blindfold. Move with the rhythm.

Experience: Visualize feminine faces; mother and child; people hugging; separation; people waving goodbye; walls being built; slaying dragons; young people going off to war; school scenes; destruction of nature. If you choose, continue listening to the next track. When complete, open your eyes and recount your visions.

Passage 4 ~ Sexual Initiation

Ritual: Touch of Passion
Music: Natale Om, Shamanic Journey

The purpose of the "Touch of Passion" ritual is to restore the body to its natural energetic state of oneness and the conscious experience of wholeness. This ecstatic experience can be realized within 45 minutes and continue up to two hours and beyond. The ritual process moves us into a trance beyond the three-dimensional world. In trance we exorcise the anger, alienation, distance and separation accumulated from the traumas of living a life that requires us to withhold our passion. When withheld, passion manifests anger and anger is the root of many diseases. Passion is essential to life and as needed as water and air. Passion is the source of life. It must be respected, not feared. Passion must be expressed and shared.

The "Touch of Passion" is an energy ritual, an intentional healing exchange between giver and receiver. There is no sexual foreplay or penetration, only the touching, pumping and moving of the receiver's body. I am unaware of anything like it, which is why it was created.

Experience: The receiver lies on their back in an open posture with arms and legs uncrossed. They close their eyes and wear a blindfold to support their inner journey, taking deep inhales through the nose with exhales through the mouth. In the first part, passion is awakened by moving energy up from our root chakra through the sacral and solar plexus to gather at the heart. To free blocked or withheld passion, moving to the rhythms of shamanic drumming, the giver uses their hands to work the receiver's body from the inner thighs up to the heart space. A natural flow of energy vibrates throughout the body as we connect with the source of our aliveness.

The second part of the ritual expands the awakened cumulated passion, with a flow of orgasmic energy, from the heart space throughout the body. This flow of energy is allowed and encouraged until it brings life to the denied and blocked parts of the receiver's body. Continuing to ride their breath, the receiver experiences a release of withheld emotions, spontaneous laughter, and the phenomenon of a continuous flow of orgasmic energy. As the ritual concludes, the receiver emerges in a deep vibrational trance, relaxed yet highly energized.

Ritual: Trance Dance
Music: Rites of Passage, "Follow Your Passion"

Find a quiet place where you won't be disturbed. Stand relaxed and ground your feet. Begin the breath of fire technique: two quick inhales through the nose and one exhale through the mouth. Play the music. Close your eyes and/or wear a blindfold. Move with the rhythm.

Experience: Visualize ecstatic images; the goddess of creation and destruction; kundalini energy rising up through your body; spirit animals; tribal fertility rites. When complete, open your eyes and recount your visions.

Passage 5 ~ Alliance with the Masculine

Ritual: Letting It Go
Music: Natale Om

Lie down on your back in an open position, arms and hands to the side with feet and legs uncrossed. Play the music. Close and/or cover your eyes, bringing attention to your breath, relaxing with each exhale.

Experience: As you breathe become clear about your intention and review the ways in which you may have surrendered your feminine values (nurturing, compassion, cooperation, etc.) in order to survive in our male dominant culture. Review all of the times you said "yes" when you wanted to say "no." All of the times you agreed when you truly did not agree; all of the times you felt dominated or even abused by the effects of male domination.

Recall moments when you may have surrendered to male domination. Take five deep circular breaths with extended exhales. With each exhale, tell yourself: "Let all that go."

After these five breaths notice if anything remains to be released. If so, take a deep breath and exhale making a sound that represents: "Let it ALL go." If the sound is negative, angry or sad, continue to breathe and release. Repeat until the sound is relaxed and peaceful and therefore complete.

Now lie there relaxed, integrating your experience until you feel like getting up.

Ritual: Trance Dance
Music: Rites of Passage, "Pass the Test"

Find a quiet place where you won't be disturbed. Stand relaxed and ground your feet. Begin the breath of fire technique: two quick inhales through the nose and one exhale through the mouth. Play the music. Close your eyes and/or wear a blindfold. Move with the rhythm.

Experience: Visualize ships; soldiers at war; workers in fields and factories; a busy city at rush hour; crowded freeways; government; corporations; sporting events; a graduation ceremony; family snapshots and home videos. When complete, open your eyes and recount your visions.

Passage 6 ~ Realization of Betrayal

Ritual: Bonding
Music: Natale Om, Shamanic Journey

Humans bond the moment after birth when placed in the arms of our mother. Until birth we had no experience of separation. We were one within our mother, an actual physical part of her. At birth we experience separation for the first time.

Bonding is essential. As an infant we felt total trust and connection with our mother. Any feeling of separation disappeared when she held us. In those bonded moments we experienced what we look for, as adults, with lovers and partners – the security and trust of infancy. Someone who will be there for us. Someone who will not betray us.

You must share this ritual with a partner you trust. Do not attempt it alone. Your thoughts and emotions need to be expressed with one or more people otherwise the ritual will reinforce self-defeating thoughts such as: "When I tell the truth people leave."

Experience: You need a secure, quiet place where you can scream and shout for about 45 minutes. Remove jewelry and accessories. Dress comfortably. Play the music. Sit on the floor facing your partner with your right leg under their left leg and your left leg over their right. Wrap your arms around each other. Pull your chest and pelvic area close. Hold each other. At first this position may give rise to sexual feelings and thoughts. These usually go away once you begin releasing.

Cover your eyes with a bandana or blindfold. While holding each other, tilt your head back to extend your neck and throat. Begin to breath consciously, deeply in through the nose allowing the exhale to become a sound, a sigh and eventually a scream or shout.

You will find this comes easily, until the anger runs out. What needs to come up is your sadness and pain. That's what you want to release. Pain is the glue that holds anger in place. You must have the courage to go through your fear to reach the anger. Anger and pain are stored in layers, one on top of the other. Anger must be pushed out consciously to create an opening that allows the pain to just flow out.

Fear > Anger/Pain > Anger/Pain > Pain

It is the pain at the source of our anger that is primary. Anger came after we were hurt as a reaction to the pain, so anger is secondary. It's important to not just scream or shout, but to allow the pain to come up. Continue to do this until you and your partner feel complete. You both will feel lighter, euphoric and grateful.

Ritual: Trance Dance
Music: Rites of Passage, "Nothing is Sacred"

Find a quiet place where you won't be disturbed. Stand relaxed and ground your feet. Begin the breath of fire technique: two quick inhales through the nose and one exhale through the mouth. Play the music. Close your eyes and/or wear a blindfold. Move with the rhythm.

Experience: Visualize happy faces transform into distrustful images; people turn their back and walk away; searching for someone to hold on to, people move out of reach; destruction of nature; faces of famous people who lied and betrayed us. When complete, open your eyes and recount your visions.

Passage 7 ~ Mid-Birth

Ritual: Celebration

Throw a party to celebrate your mid-birth (39th birthday) or that of a friend or loved one. Everyone who has recently completed mid-birth should be acknowledged, treated like royalty and given what they want. Grant them three wishes possible within the context of the celebration. Once the celebrities have been sufficiently pampered, play a fun ritual game I learned in Mexico to honor this passage.

Invite the three or four youngest people at the party to sit in a row of chairs. The honored mid-birthers form a line to the right of the seated young people.

Next, one by one, the mid-birth celebrities step forward and bend over. In turn, each young person ritually spanks them. The other party goers join in mocking the celebrities by pointing fingers and having fun with them.

This is done as pay back for those celebrities who for years may have acted like they knew everything, who now say they are confused and know nothing. This ritual should always be enjoyed in the spirit of good fun and playfulness.

Ritual: Trance Dance
Music: Rites of Passage, "Home to Heal"

Find a quiet place where you won't be disturbed. Stand relaxed and ground your feet. Begin the breath of fire technique: two quick inhales through the nose and one exhale through the mouth. Play the music. Close your eyes and/or wear a blindfold. Move with the rhythm.

Experience: Visualize resurrection; time lapse photography of blooming flowers; butterflies emerging from cocoons; chicks breaking out of eggs; sunrise; an erupting volcano; people celebrating in spiritual dance. When complete, open your eyes and recount your visions.

Passage 8 ~ Re-connection with the Feminine

Ritual: Soul Hunting
Music: Natale Om

Lie on your back in the open position with arms and legs uncrossed. Close and/or cover your eyes. Bring your attention to your breath. Breathe deeply, in and out. As you exhale allow yourself to fall deeper into trance.

Experience: While breathing, begin to think of all the ways you may have sacrificed your integrity to be successful in the world of the masculine. Imagine you have a huge net or you are in a flying ship with huge sails traveling across the universe.

As you travel, collect all the times you may have compromised yourself or your integrity in order to be successful, dominate and win. Recognize the times you ignored or failed to follow your dreams. Catch all of these moments in your net or snag them in your sail so they fall onto the deck of your flying ship.

When we compromise ourself or our dreams we lose or reject a part of our authentic self. When you have collected as many soul parts as you can, see them as times when you surrendered yourself or your soul. Gather all of these lost pieces and place them in your heart.

As these lost pieces enter your heart, feel them push all of the darkness that has taken their place, out of your body and mind. Feel all the egotistical and unnatural behavior leave. Allow the returning soul parts to completely clear your heart of darkness. When you feel complete, take your non-dominant hand and place it gently over your heart. Welcome home those lost pieces of self.

When you are ready, return to normal consciousness. You may want to lie there for a while. When you do get up, you may feel very relaxed. This is the peace that comes when we replace darkness with light, when we feel complete.

Ritual: Trance Dance
Music: Rites of Passage, "Mother of All"

Find a quiet place where you won't be disturbed. Stand relaxed and ground your feet. Begin the breath of fire technique: two quick inhales through the nose and one exhale through the mouth. Play the music. Close your eyes and/or wear a blindfold. Move with the rhythm.

Experience: Visualize scenes of natural beauty; mother and child; flying through the air; peaceful activities like sailing, meditating, floating in a pool of water; young children running into the arms of their Mother; people hugging; clouds adrift in a blue sky. When complete, open your eyes and recount your visions.

Passage 9 ~ Initiation into the Truth

Ritual: The Truth Stick

With a group of people, create a circle large enough for someone to stand inside. Place a "truth stick" in the center of the circle. This is usually a tree branch a meter long decorated with feathers, beads, and other power symbols. Otherwise, use what you have, but give the stick your full attention. Everyone sits and each person has one chance to enter the circle, stand and: "Speak a truth, which is true for everyone."

Once someone has spoken members of the circle may challenge what was said – if they think it was just the speaker's truth and not an absolute truth. All members of the circle are not required to enter the circle and are allowed to pass.

This ritual can be very short if no one steps into the circle and attempts to speak the truth. If this happens, the facilitator invites everyone to sit in silence for a while. If no one takes the opportunity to speak, the facilitator shares: "What this demonstrates is we should realize that we are incapable of speaking the truth. We are only able to speak our truth, which is only our point of view and not true for everyone." Then have an open discussion, absent of judgment.

Ritual: Trance Dance
Music: Rites of Passage, "Truth's Vibration"

Find a quiet place where you won't be disturbed. Stand relaxed and ground your feet. Begin the breath of fire technique: two quick inhales through the nose and one exhale through the mouth. Play the music. Close your eyes and/or wear a blindfold. Move with the rhythm.

Experience: Visualize white light; scenes from different religious rituals and ceremonies; court room in session; war room in session; demonstrations; famous politicians, scientists and revolutionaries. When complete, open your eyes and recount your visions.

Passage 10 ~ Atonement

Ritual: Forgiveness and Being

Invite a partner to read this guided visualization or record it yourself and use it whenever needed. I recommend you do this experience more than once, but never more than once in a day.

Close your eyes and relax. Imagine a horizon and you are standing on it. Create your Mother walking toward you. Have her stand in front of you, allowing you to be and allowing her to be.

Create your Father walking toward you. Have him stand in front of you, allowing you to be and allowing him to be.

Now create your lover walking toward you. Have them stand in front of you, allowing you to be and allowing them to be.

Gaze into your Mother's eyes, allowing her to just be and experience her allowing you to be. Repeat the following questions 3 times, being sure to pause about 5 seconds between each.

- What did you do with your Mother?
- What did you do to your Mother?
- What did your Mother do to you?
- What did your Mother teach you about men?
- What did your Mother teach you about women?
- Who's been doing your relating?

Gaze into your Father's eyes, allowing him to just be and experience him allowing you to be. Repeat the following questions 3 times, being sure to pause about 5 seconds between each.

- What did you do with your Father?
- What did you do to your Father?
- What did your Father do to you?
- What did your Father teach you about women?
- What did your father teach you about men?
- Who's been doing your relating?

Gaze into your lover's eyes, allowing them to be and experience them allowing you to be. Repeat the following questions 3 times, being sure to pause about 5 seconds between each.

- What did your Mother teach you about relating to women?
- What did your Father teach you about relating to men?
- What did your Mother teach you about relating to men?
- What did your Father teach you about relating to women?
- Who's been doing your relating?

Are you willing to take responsibility for your relationship with your parents?

What circumstances are you unwilling to take responsibility for?

What's keeping you from having a complete relationship with your parents?

Gaze into the eyes of your Mother.

- What are you willing to forgive your Mother for?
- What else are you now willing to forgive your Mother for?
- With your Mother, for what are you now willing to accept her forgiveness?
- Now let go of your Mother and allow her to be.

Gaze into the eyes of your Father.

- What are you willing to forgive your Father for?
- What else are you now willing to forgive your Father for?
- With your Father, for what are you now willing to accept his forgiveness?
- Now let go of your Father and allow him to be.

Gaze into the eyes of your lover.

- What are you willing to forgive your lover for?
- What else are you now willing to forgive your Lover for?
- With your lover, for what are you now willing to accept their forgiveness?
- Now let go of your lover and allow them to be.

Now look at your parents. Allow them to be and experience them allowing you to be.

- What are you willing to forgive your parents for?
- What else are you now willing to forgive your parents for?
- What are you willing to accept forgiveness for from your parents?
- What else are you now willing to accept forgiveness for from your parents?

Create space around your Mother, Father and lover.

- Now be with them and just allow them to be.
- Experience them allowing you to be.
- Experience them creating you just the way you are.
- Allow yourself to experience loving them.
- Experience them loving you.

- Expand that love so anything can happen within
  the relationship.

Now say what you want to say to them.

Now say what you are hesitant to say to them.

Now say what you always wanted to say, but were afraid of the consequences.

Now say what you always wanted to say, but were embarrassed to say it.

Is there something you want to say, that you don't want to say?

SAY IT!

Now say everything you want to say. (pause)

Now realize you will never say it all and say that.

Now just look at them. Atone with them. Become their vibration, allow them to just be and experience them allowing you to be.

Now let them go. Complete this gathering. Complete this relationship.

How they go and how you complete this relationship is totally up to you. It is within your power to complete this relationship any way you choose. (pause about two minutes)

Now open your eyes. Allow everyone to just be and experience them allowing you to be.

Ritual: Trance Dance
Music: Rites of Passage, "Atone"

Find a quiet place where you won't be disturbed. Stand relaxed and ground your feet. Begin the breath of fire technique: two quick inhales through the nose and one exhale through the mouth. Play the music. Close your eyes and/or wear a blindfold. Move with the rhythm.

Experience: Visualize images of twins; bells ringing; similar-looking family members; elderly couples; people smiling and laughing; people chanting. When complete, open your eyes and recount your visions.

Passage 11 ~ Elderhood

Ritual: Faces of Time
Music: Natale Om, Flying Om

Dim the lights. Play the music. Sit opposite a partner on the floor in a simple cross-legged position. Do not hold your knees or support yourself with your hands and arms. Place some pillows or blankets behind you. Have a bandana or blindfold handy to cover your eyes. Set a timer to ring in 15 minutes.

Experience: Gaze at your partner's face in an open and receptive manner. Breathe fully and deeply, in through the nose and exhale through the mouth. Your eyes will tend to close once they begin to see your partner's face change. Keep them open. Sometimes the face changes into someone else or will just distort and move. Keep your eyes open the full 15 minutes.

When the timer sounds, close your eyes and cover them with the bandanna or blindfold. Begin the breath of fire: two quick inhales through the nose and one exhale through the mouth. When you feel the need, take a deep breath and hold it as long as you can, then exhale fully and slowly contract your stomach. Return to the breath of fire. When you feel moved, allow yourself to fall backward onto the pillows.

When you return to normal consciousness, share your experience with your partner. If you return before your partner, do not speak to them or interrupt them. After an appropriate time has passed, invite them back by gently touching their hand or elbow.

Ritual: Time Capsule

One of the qualifications for being a teaching elder is to know and continue the quest to know oneself. When exploring distant planets, the NASA program carries recorded sounds and symbols that could inform intelligent life how 21ST Century humanity views life on earth. Included are music, different languages, images of parents, children, trees, animals, etc.

Experience: Create a collection of personal items that express who you are and what your life means. What symbolizes how you value your relationships? What do your children mean to you? How would you symbolize your career, your dreams, your qualities and skills? Collect these revealing and treasured objects and make a shadow box display. Or, create a collage made from photographs and magazine clippings that represent your life and values.

Ritual: Trance Dance
Music: Rites of Passage, "Inner Horizon"

Find a quiet place where you won't be disturbed. Stand relaxed and ground your feet. Begin the breath of fire technique: two quick inhales through the nose and one exhale through the mouth. Play the music. Close your eyes and/or wear a blindfold. Move with the rhythm.

Experience: Visualize traveling through different worlds or realities; pictures of wise elders of all time; surreal natural environments; floating in space. When complete, open your eyes and recount your visions.

Passage 12 ~ Sharing Your Wisdom

Ritual: Mentoring

In every community there is a great need for mentors and coaches to share their wisdom and experience. Inquire about opportunities to volunteer through your local school, community center, service center or religious group. Middle-school students, dealing with the radical changes of their "Coming of Age" passage, are especially in need of guidance and support. Consider the difference you will make sharing your life skills – art, personal finance, creative writing, gardening, fitness, sports, etc. – and encouraging children to take responsibility for their lives and education.

There are countless mentoring organizations focused on leadership and service. Sharing your wisdom may be the most satisfying and rewarding experience of your life. Explore the possibilities.

Ritual: Sharing in the City

This ritual will be easy for some people and a challenge for others. If difficult, stick with it and overcome your avoidance.

Go to a public place where people gather like a park or a shopping mall. Avoid service people who may be working and are required to speak with you.

Approach someone you do not know who appears friendly. Say hello and begin a conversation about something you have in common or can observe. When they are receptive, create the opportunity to share your story and for them to share with you. If appropriate, exchange contact information.

Do this for a few weeks until you are comfortable with the process. The lesson is to not take the experience of rejection personally, but to see that as someone else's choice. If you are shy or reluctant, accept that is also a choice. There are always other ways to share your story in meaningful ways.

Passage 13 ~ Beyond Duality

The following are rituals you may use to look at your own death and resurrection. It is helpful to invite a friend or partner to take turns reading the visualizations then share your experiences after both of you have completed.

Ritual: Your Obituary

Close your eyes, relax and recall the major events of your life: your accomplishments, the things in life for which you want to be remembered. Include the future and plans or goals yet to be accomplished.

Now, in the third person, write about yourself as if you have died. Create a descriptive account of your life up until your death. Describe how you die and your age at death.

Now, ask yourself, "Does this describe what I want from my life?" If the answer is "yes" no further comment is necessary. If the answer is "no" rewrite the obituary to describe ideally how you choose to live and be remembered.

Now write a short epitaph that sums up the life you have lived and expect to live. For examples: "Did not join. Did not follow. Did not lead." or "Loving parent. True friend."

Ritual: Death Bed Scene

Find a quiet place where you can sit or lie down without being inter-rupted. Imagine yourself very old and on your deathbed. Close your eyes and allow your life, from beginning to the present, to pass before you. Take deep breaths and relax as you view your life. After three to five minutes, consider these questions and, if you want, make notes in your journal:

What memories bring you the most pain? What memories bring you the most pleasure?

What experiences, commitments and accomplishments have given meaning to your life?

Do you have any regrets? If so, what could you have done differently?

What can you do differently now?

Do you wish you had spent more time with anyone?

Do you wish you had spent less time with anyone?

What were the choices you feared?

What were the choices you were unaware of?

Did you discover what you value?

Are your values what you want them to be?

Have you discovered something you want to change?

If yes make the conscious commitment now to change it. Return to normal consciousness.

Ritual: Your Last Hour

Sit or lie down in a place where you will not be interrupted. Consider your life. Imagine you have one hour to live and you can spend that hour with anyone.

Who would that be?

How and where would you spend this last hour?

Does the person or persons know you feel this way?

Close your eyes and breathe deeply. Make the conscious commitment now to let this person know how you feel. Return to normal consciousness.

Ritual: Returning to the Elements
Music: Natale Om

Invite a partner to read this visualization experience for you. Play the music softly enough so the partner can be heard. Lie on your back with your eyes closed, hands and feet uncrossed. Become still. Bring your attention to your breath and allow yourself to relax.

Experience: Imagine it is summer. You're barefoot and walking on the warm earth. A bright sun warms your body and face. You walk into a beautiful meadow with wild flowers, birds singing and butterflies everywhere.

You lie down and feel the warmth of the earth coming into you. The heat of the sun covers the top of your body.

Notice the difference, the closeness of the Great Mother's warmth while Father Sun warms you from a distance.

Allow your thoughts to just run their course, coming and going. Don't hold on to any of them. Let them all go. (Pause)

Now begin to feel a warm breeze running over the upper part of your body. Feel the breeze become cooler while the earth remains warm beneath you.

Summer passes, the breeze grows cooler. Mother Earth remains warm. The warmth and light of Father Sun becomes less. He is moving away, as fathers do.

Leaves begin to fall. The leaves fall from the trees and cover your body creating a blanket that holds you close to the warmth of the Mother and protects you from the autumn chill.

Winter arrives with a cool purifying snow. The snow covers the leaves. You're still protected by the blanket of leaves that hold you close to the warmth of the Mother.

The weather grows cooler and cooler. You become very still, almost frozen. Then you begin to feel movement beneath and around you.

This is life. It is springtime. You and the earth around you become warmer. The snow melts and the roots of plants start to grow around you.

The Mother is getting warmer as the Father begins to return, until it is summer once again.

Season upon season, layer upon layer, you go deeper and deeper into the earth. Leaves upon the earth, snow upon leaves, deeper and deeper you go. (Pause)

Arrive at a place where you are totally still, a place where you are totally at peace. Stay in this still and peaceful place. (Pause)

Open your eyes and stretch. Welcome back to the magic. Consider the following:

How will your next life be different? How will it look? Create your future. Create your next life now.

Ritual: Trance Dance
Music: Rites of Passage, "Final Passage" followed by "Dance the Day Away"

Stand relaxed and ground your feet. Begin the breath of fire technique: two quick inhales through the nose and one exhale through the mouth. Play the music. Close your eyes and/or wear a blindfold. Move with the rhythm.

Experience: Visualize angels; a tunnel of white light, ascending from the earth into the heavens; your body transforming into light and energy; entering other life forms; babies being born; dancing in the light; being greeted by the souls on the other side; being held in the arms of the Great Mother. When complete, open your eyes and recount your visions.

For more, visit FrankNatale.com

CPSIA information can be obtained
at www.ICGtesting.com
Printed in the USA
JSHW050957210621
16055JS00002B/139